THE GOURMET KITCHEN

THE GOURMET KITCHEN

Recipes from the Creator of Savory Simple

JENNIFER FARLEY

GALLERY BOOKS

NEW YORK   LONDON   TORONTO   SYDNEY   NEW DELHI

G

Gallery Books
An Imprint of Simon & Schuster, Inc.
1230 Avenue of the Americas
New York, NY 10020

First Gallery Books trade paperback edition October 2016

GALLERY BOOKS and colophon are registered trademarks of Simon & Schuster, Inc.

For information about special discounts for bulk purchases, please contact Simon & Schuster Special Sales at 1-866-506-1949 or business@simonandschuster.com.

The Simon & Schuster Speakers Bureau can bring authors to your live event. For more information or to book an event, contact the Simon & Schuster Speakers Bureau at 1-866-248-3049 or visit our website at www.simonspeakers.com.

Design by Jaime Putorti

Manufactured in the United States of America

10 9 8 7 6 5 4 3 2 1

Library of Congress Cataloging-in-Publication Data

Names: Farley, Jennifer, 1978– author.
Title: The gourmet kitchen : recipes from the creator of Savory Simple /
  Jennifer Farley.
Description: First Gallery Books trade paperback edition. | New York :
  Gallery Books, 2016. | Series: Gallery original nonfiction trade
Identifiers: LCCN 2016017323
Subjects: LCSH: Cooking. | LCGFT: Cookbooks.
Classification: LCC TX714 .F367 2016 | DDC 641.5—dc23
LC record available at https://lccn.loc.gov/2016017323

ISBN 978-1-5011-0257-8
ISBN 978-1-5011-0258-5 (ebook)

— This book is dedicated to my family —

CONTENTS

SOUPS AND SALADS

APPETIZERS AND SIDES

MAIN COURSES

SWEETS AND TREATS

I was thirty-two when I started cooking; up until then, I just ate.
—Julia Child

INTRODUCTION

I grew up in Columbia, Maryland, a suburb directly between Baltimore and Washington, DC, in the 1980s. Food wasn't a defining part of my childhood, but as necessity would have it, it was always there. Some of my earliest memories involve food: watching my mother bake elaborate cakes from a 1950s Betty Crocker booklet, snacking on astronaut ice cream at the Baltimore Science Center, and learning how to bake mandel bread with my grandma, Zelda. One time I asked her what the difference was between mandel bread and biscotti and her reply was "Jennifer, Jewish people don't eat biscotti." I wasn't a picky eater; that was my brother, Dave. I basically liked to eat everything. I loved Grandma's chocolate pistachio cake. My stranger-danger protection plan was simple: I wasn't allowed to get into a car with someone unless they knew the magic words "blintz soufflé."

Compared to many people, I've led an incredibly easy life. However, I struggled to get where I am today due to years of battling with bipolar II depression, crippling anxieties, and overwhelming career indecisiveness. I wasn't one of those kids who always knew what she wanted to be when she grew up. It's astounding to think that the answer was always right there in front of me. I was just looking at it from the wrong angle.

I spent most of my twenties agonizing over my career. I graduated from Towson University in 2000 with a bachelor's degree in English and no real ambition. I was an English major because I loved reading and writing, not because I wanted to be a professor. I took a job at my family's business, a photography company. Initially, I worked as one of the photographers, but soon switched gears and got Microsoft certified. I returned to the family business soon after, this time in the position of network administrator. It was a job I stuck with for almost ten years. During this time I taught myself Photoshop and became the company's image editor. In addition to learning how to edit photos, I got my first hand-me-down SLR camera and began shooting as a hobby photographer on the side. So to review: English degree, network administrator, graphic artist, hobby photographer. I was a jack-of-all-trades.

As time passed, I realized that I was not happy spending eight hours at a desk every day. Over the next several years, I went back to school multiple times and always quit soon after I realized I was headed in the wrong direction yet again. I frustrated loved ones (and myself) with my indecisiveness. I contemplated various career paths, and there were times where something would ignite a spark for a few months, but that spark never survived. I felt helpless, but I had also become fixated on the notion that I would never be completely happy unless I was passionate about my career. I knew there was something out there, that *one thing* that would bring me satisfaction.

Food was becoming a huge part of my life, as I dined out regularly with friends, tried new cuisines, began taking cooking classes, and found myself glued to the Travel Channel and Food Network where celebrity chefs like Anthony Bourdain and Andrew Zimmern waxed poetic about Icelandic lamb and the street food scene in Osaka. I wanted to see the world and eat it, too.

When I wasn't watching shows about food and travel, I was reading. I plowed my way through the food memoir section at my local bookstore. I read Ruth Reichl's *Garlic and Sapphires,* and was filled with daydreams of becoming a professional restaurant critic. I read Anthony Bourdain's *Kitchen Confidential* followed by Bill Buford's *Heat,* and began wondering what it would be like to work the line in a restaurant. When I read Julia Child's *My Life in France,* everything changed. Not overnight. It was a slow, gradual shift.

I connected with Julia's story. I saw myself in her gleeful delight over small details such as a beautiful Paris neighborhood or a delicious butter sauce. Julia enrolled in Le Cordon Bleu at age thirty-seven. I was twenty-nine and wanted to learn to be an amazing cook. Finally, after a lot of debate and many skeptical looks from friends and family, I decided to leave my job and attend culinary school. If Julia could do it, so could I. It was one of the most emotionally intense and challenging experiences of my life, but the techniques I learned at school and working in restaurants were invaluable. I got to experience firsthand some of what Julia wrote about in her memoir. I felt the frantic pressure of the line that Bill Buford so accurately describes in his memoir *Heat.* I also began to resent one of my former inspirations, Anthony Bourdain, when he stated that no one over thirty should attend culinary school. My defiance at that statement pushed me to work harder.

In September 2009, three months before heading to L'Academie de Cuisine, I started my blog, *Savory Simple.* After reading Kathleen Flinn's memoir, *The Sharper Your*

Knife, the Less You Cry, and S. J. Sebellin-Ross's blog, *Cooking School Confidential,* I felt compelled to document my experience. I wanted a creative outlet, a place to share recipes and connect with like-minded people. Maybe I would inspire someone else to chase their dreams. I had no idea the blog would ultimately blossom into a career and lead to so many incredible opportunities. The journey I've been on has been a whirlwind.

This book is a compilation of recipes both old and new, and they showcase the food I've grown to love. Some have been in my family for generations, like my grandmother's crab cakes. I've found inspiration everywhere from culinary school to my travels around the world. Several of these recipes are from my blog, while others are adapted from cookbooks and chefs who have inspired me over the years. Most of them have evolved through experimenting with the techniques I learned in culinary school. I consider many of these recipes to be geared toward special occasion cooking, such as casual dinner parties, a leisurely weekend meal, or a romantic dinner for two. These are everyday gourmet recipes for the home cook.

Cooking presents a great opportunity for creativity in the kitchen, and many of the ingredients in this book can be treated as suggestions rather than hard-and-fast must-haves. What tastes good to me might be overly salty to you. Learn to refine your palate and experiment with different flavors. Love garlic? Add more. Hate it? Do yourself a favor and omit it completely. Swap out certain ingredients. I repeatedly mention five tastes throughout this book: sweet, salty, bitter, sour, and umami. The best dishes have a proper balance of these tastes. Use that knowledge to your advantage.

Understand that experimentation, mistakes, and kitchen failures are part of becoming a better cook. Even though baking is more precise, that doesn't mean you can't still experiment. Swap out the strawberries with your favorite berry. Learn about complementary flavors; try adding some fresh herbs or your favorite spice. Do a bit of research before you begin experimenting. Accept that experiments aren't always successful, but that sometimes risk leads to great reward.

Always read the entire recipe before getting started. Read it twice if you're as scatterbrained as I am. Make sure you have all of your ingredients and equipment. Make sure the baking powder hasn't expired. If a recipe has many complex steps and takes time, see if you can start it the day before. Anything that needs to chill, such as tart dough, can be made in advance.

Above all else, have fun with it!

INGREDIENTS AND EQUIPMENT

INGREDIENTS

This is not an exhaustive list of ingredients used in the book. However, most of these ingredients lay the foundation for my recipes, so it's important to understand product variations, quality, and best buying practices.

ALCOHOL. I cook and bake with a lot of booze, including hard liquor, wine, and sweet liqueurs. If you prefer to cook without alcohol, you can omit it and substitute with another ingredient. For baked goods, increase one of the other listed liquids (such as dairy) by the same amount being subtracted so that it's an even swap. Substitute stock or water in recipes where alcohol is used to deglaze.

AROMATICS (ONIONS, SHALLOTS, GARLIC, SCALLIONS, LEEKS, AND CHIVES). Aromatics are an essential part of cooking. When a recipe calls for cooked onions, I almost always use yellow onions because I think they have the most well-balanced flavor profile. For recipes using raw onions, I typically use red onions. Shallots are an excellent substitute for red onions if you prefer a milder flavor. Caramelizing or roasting aromatics is one of my favorite ways to enhance a savory recipe.

BUTTER. I always use unsalted butter when cooking or baking. Clarified butter (also known as ghee) is unsalted butter with the milk solids removed. It is a great option for grilling or sautéing, because it has a high smoke point unlike regular butter. Ghee can be found in the international aisle of many grocery stores. Finally, several recipes call for brown butter. Though it can be intimidating to make at first, it's not difficult.

BUTTERMILK. Buttermilk adds a wonderful softness and tanginess to recipes. I typically purchase buttermilk, but in a pinch you can make it from scratch. Add 1 tablespoon of fresh-squeezed lemon juice or white vinegar to 1 cup of whole milk and allow the mixture to sit until it curdles, about 10 minutes.

CHEESE. As it does with so many foods, quality makes all of the difference when it comes to cheese. Fresh cheeses, preferably with the rind attached, are the best (pre-grated cheeses are full of fillers and chemicals). Grate or cut just before serving. I promise, you'll be able to taste the difference in freshness.

CHILI PEPPERS. I often use serrano, jalapeño, and poblano peppers, serrano being the hottest of the three. Each pepper can range from spicy to bland, so it's not a bad idea to taste a small piece before adding it to a recipe. The hottest parts of these peppers are the seeds and ribs, so remove them completely for less heat. If a recipe calls for poblano peppers but you want no heat at all, green bell peppers are a great substitute. I recommend wearing food-safe gloves when working with hot peppers.

CHOCOLATE. As I've said before, ingredient quality can make a huge difference in recipes. For convenience purposes, I often still choose standard grocery store brands when it's time to temper chocolate, but will only use high-quality unsweetened cocoa powder for baking. I recommend Valrhona for rich flavor and potent color.

CITRUS. I always keep lemons and limes in the refrigerator, ready to use as needed. The juice can be used to brighten up sauces, roasted vegetables, vinaigrettes, soups, and more. Oranges are sweeter and less acidic but can be used in the same way. Grapefruit is wonderful for adding both sweetness and bitterness. Citrus zest can also be used to add flavor to many dishes. When possible, always use fresh-squeezed juice (especially with lemons and limes) for best taste.

COCONUT MILK. I prefer using canned coconut milk, and I strongly recommend using full fat over light or reduced-fat coconut milk. It has a better flavor and consistency.

CRÈME FRAÎCHE AND SOUR CREAM. Crème fraîche and sour cream are very similar, and can often be used interchangeably. Crème fraîche is thicker, richer, and less tangy than sour cream and is my preferred choice, but it's also more expensive. To save money, you can make your own crème fraîche by stirring 1 tablespoon of buttermilk or yogurt into 1 cup of heavy cream, covering the mixture, and allowing it to sit at room temperature until thick (12 to 24 hours).

EGGS. I always use large eggs. Make sure you don't accidentally purchase extra-large eggs, especially for use in baked goods. The wrong size egg, believe it or not, can have a drastic effect on the outcome of the dish.

FLOURS. I use unbleached all-purpose flour in most of my recipes, though you'll occasionally see alternatives such as whole wheat flour or almond flour. I don't typically purchase cake flour because the same effect can be achieved by decreasing the quantity of all-purpose flour and adding an equal amount of cornstarch (approximately 1 tablespoon per cup), a technique you will see in several recipes. For baked goods, you will always see both weight (ounce) and volume (cup) measurements. If you want consistent results, it is very important for you to weigh flour on a kitchen scale. Cup measurements are included, but I strongly recommend avoiding them.

GOCHUJANG. Gochujang is a wonderful chili paste used in Korean cooking. It's savory, slightly sweet, and packs a good amount of heat without being overly aggressive, so I sometimes use it in main courses. Gochujang can be found at Asian grocery stores, many online retailers, and occasionally in the international aisle of national grocery chains.

HERBS. I typically use fresh herbs, though you'll see dried herbs in recipes on occasion. If your home allows for it, you can save a lot of money by growing your own.

MILK, CREAM, AND DAIRY ALTERNATIVES. I always specify which type of milk or cream will work best in a recipe, but usually it can be swapped out with the milk of your choice (though I advise against making ice cream with anything lighter than 50 percent cream and 50 percent whole milk). Keep in mind that substitutions will alter the results. Fat often improves the flavor and texture of a recipe, but that doesn't mean it can't be lightened up. If a recipe calls for whole milk and you would prefer a lighter version, I recommend trying 2% milk. For a dairy-free version, unsweetened soy milk is often a good choice because it is richer and higher in fat than nut-based milks. Remember that when you cut down the fat in baked goods, the results typically will be drier and denser.

NUTS AND SEEDS. I usually purchase nuts and seeds raw and in bulk when possible. Store them in the freezer to keep them from going rancid.

OILS. I use a variety of oils (toasted sesame oil, coconut oil, olive oil, etc.), and there are multiple references to neutral, high-heat oils for cooking. Some great options for high-heat cooking include safflower oil, grapeseed oil, and avocado oil.

OLIVE OIL (REGULAR AND EXTRA-VIRGIN). I keep three types of olive oil in my pantry: regular olive oil, an inexpensive extra-virgin olive oil for everyday use, and a high-quality extra-virgin olive oil. Regular olive oil has a high smoke point and is a good choice for grilling directly on very high heat. I use my "everyday" extra-virgin olive oil for any instance where less intense heat will be applied such as roasting vegetables or caramelizing onions. I save the high-quality extra-virgin olive oil for raw applications where you'll really notice the flavor, such as vinaigrettes and dips.

SALT AND PEPPER. Certain recipes list specific quantities of salt and pepper, while others offer the more ambiguous "season to taste." You always want to season to taste, because your version of a properly seasoned dish might taste quite different from mine. Often when a dish tastes boring, it's because it's lacking salt. I've specified kosher salt throughout the book for consistency purposes, and because it's a great all-purpose salt for cooking and baking. However, there's nothing wrong with using sea or table salt. Remember that using different salts in recipes can alter the results. If you cook frequently and use a lot of black pepper, it's fine to purchase ground black pepper. However, if the pepper is going to sit in your spice cabinet for six months untouched, you should purchase a pepper mill and use freshly ground pepper.

SOY SAUCE AND TAMARI. These two similar ingredients should not be used interchangeably. Tamari is slightly thicker and less salty. Both add a rich, savory umami flavor to recipes.

SPICES (GROUND AND WHOLE). While I use mostly ground spices, whole spices are good for infusing flavors into certain recipes like stocks and simple syrups. Be sure to strain them out before serving.

STOCKS. Homemade stock is the essence of good soups, stews, and sauces. Store-bought versions of chicken, beef, and seafood stock are typically broths that haven't been prepared using bones. Bones contain collagen, which is used to make the gelatin found in an assortment of commercial products. This gelatinous material is what gives homemade stock that thick, rich flavor and viscous consistency found in many restaurant sauces. Not only do commercial stocks lack collagen, they are often full of additives including salt and sugar. Real stock should be salt-free, so you have the option to season your dishes to the desired level. Many recipes in this book use chicken stock, and several use seafood or vegetable stock. I'm including recipes for all three (pages 15–17). If you've never tried making it, I promise it's not difficult. If you don't want to invest the time, I often see homemade stock for sale at local meat and seafood markets. If grocery store stock is the only option, stick with a low-sodium brand, preferably one that is free of salt, sugar, chemicals, and other preservatives.

SWEETENERS. The most common sweeteners used in this book are granulated (white) sugar, light brown sugar, dark brown sugar, honey, and pure maple syrup. Always make sure you're using 100 percent honey (some manufacturers add corn syrup) and 100 percent pure maple syrup. Grade B maple syrup has more flavor, which will be more pronounced in baked goods, but Grade A is fine if it's already in your fridge.

VANILLA. Recipes in this book call for either pure vanilla extract or vanilla beans (sometimes both). I never use imitation vanilla extract, so pay attention to what you're buying. Do not buy vanilla beans from the grocery store because they are insanely overpriced; instead, purchase bulk vanilla beans online at a fraction of the price. I typically use Madagascar bourbon vanilla beans and extract.

VINEGAR. There's a noticeable difference in flavor and acidity depending on which brands of vinegar you use. It's good to experiment. I always keep a good-quality balsamic, white wine, red wine, and apple cider vinegar in my pantry.

YOGURT. I never cared for yogurt until I switched to full fat, and now that's all I use. Greek yogurt is fine, and I prefer plain. If you swap one for the other, remember that Greek yogurt has a thicker consistency and will therefore alter results.

EQUIPMENT

The quality of your kitchen tools can make or break a recipe. A simmering soup is much more likely to burn when vegetables sink to the bottom of a thin pot. That same soup will be textured or velvety depending on the pureeing power of your blender. I'm not suggesting that you go out and spend thousands of dollars to upgrade all of your kitchen equipment at once. But if you love to cook, it's great to invest over time in sturdy, well-made equipment.

2-QUART STAINLESS STEEL SAUCEPAN. This is my second most used pot. I have an All-Clad, but Cuisinart, Calphalon, and Anolon are also good options (I recommend the same brands for the skillets and sautoir referenced on the following pages). This heavy-bottom saucepan is the perfect size for grains, sauces, browning butter, simple syrup, ice cream base, curds, and caramel. It's also a good size base to use as a double boiler.

BENCH SCRAPER. A bench scraper is a rectangular tool that's very useful for working with dough. It can be used to cut, divide, and lift thinly rolled-out dough. Some bench scrapers also include ruler markings, making it a great multitasking kitchen tool.

BLENDER. I'm not going to tell you that a four-hundred-dollar blender is a kitchen essential. However, if you prepare homemade soups, the difference between a Vitamix and the more standard home models is significant. The Vitamix will give your pureed soups an incredibly smooth, silky consistency. I also use it for smoothies, vinaigrettes, and an assortment of purees and drinks.

CHEF'S KNIFE. I have many knives (including a paring knife, a serrated knife, and a slicer), but if you're going to invest in one good-quality knife, make it an eight-inch or ten-inch chef's knife. Keep it sharp. Some of my favorite brands are Wüsthof, Global, and Hammer Stahl.

DIGITAL SCALE. Do not bake without a scale. Seriously. A scale guarantees consistent results that you will never see if you use measuring cups, especially with flour. A cup of flour might weigh anywhere from 3½ to 5 ounces, depending on how it's measured. If you spoon the flour into the cup it will weigh less than if you scoop the cup into the flour bin. Trust me, that extra flour will make a big difference in the density of your cake, or how wide your cookies spread in the oven.

DIGITAL THERMOMETER. I use the same inexpensive corded probe digital thermometer for both cooking meat and candy making. It takes all the guesswork out of cooking meat to its proper internal temperature.

ENAMELED CAST-IRON DUTCH OVEN. I use my 4½-quart Dutch oven more than any other pot in the kitchen. It's a sturdy, even conductor of heat and can replace my skillet, saucepan, and sautoir in a pinch. I use it mainly for soups and stews, but it's also great for searing meats, cooking pasta, and blanching vegetables. If you are short on space or can only afford to buy one nice pot, this should be it. Le Creuset and Lodge both offer excellent options.

FOOD MILL. Very few recipes in this book call for a food mill. I probably only use mine a few times per year, but there's no other tool that gets the job done nearly as well when I need it. A food mill purees soft food (think sauces and soups) while straining out fiber, seeds, and skin. It's faster and easier than combining ingredients in a blender and then forcing everything through a strainer.

FOOD PROCESSOR. I have a classic Cuisinart food processor and I use it for dips, grating cheese, chopping nuts, making pie and tart dough as well as homemade nut butters, and combining ingredients for breakfast bars.

FRENCH ROLLING PIN. I recommend using French rolling pins instead of the more standard cylindrical rolling pins with handles. A French rolling pin tapers down at the sides and you use it by gently pressing on the ends while rolling. This gives you more control over the dough. Don't wash the rolling pin after using it. Scrape off excess dough using a bench scraper.

HEAT-RESISTANT SPATULA. I no longer use wooden spoons. Heat-resistant silicone spatulas can go right in the dishwasher.

HEAT-RESISTANT TONGS. I primarily use kitchen tongs for handling hot food and tossing pasta and salad ingredients.

ICE CREAM MACHINE. There are tutorials on the Web for making ice cream without a machine. However, I find it to be a cumbersome process and the results are not always consistent. Reasonably priced ice cream machines are available, and I use mine all the time during hot summer months. Once you master homemade ice cream, it's the easiest thing in the world and the ultimate crowd pleaser when guests arrive. I use a Cuisinart ice cream maker, but there are plenty of other good brands. Make sure to freeze the attachment overnight. I also recommend chilling the ice cream base overnight if you have enough time.

KITCHEN GLOVES. Keep kitchen gloves on hand, specifically for dealing with hot peppers and handling items that can cause discoloration like beets and cherries. Sometimes I also use them when handling raw chicken.

MICROPLANE ZESTER. I use my microplane for zesting citrus, grating fresh nutmeg, and occasionally for grating cheese over pasta.

SHEET PANS AND FITTED PARCHMENT SHEETS. I use sheet pans, which are found in commercial kitchens and can be purchased inexpensively online. Sheet pans come in a few sizes but I keep two sizes on hand: half-sheet pans and full-sheet pans. A half-sheet pan is good for smaller quantities such as roasted vegetables. A full-sheet pan basically takes up an entire oven shelf so it's useful for baking a lot of cookies at once. The best thing about using commercial sheet pans is that you can also buy inexpensive packs of parchment sheets that are exactly the same size (also available online). It's much easier to use those than to deal with the rolled parchment sold at grocery stores. Rounded parchment sheets for cake pans are also available online.

STAINLESS STEEL AND NONSTICK SKILLETS. I have a few different skillets, but I use an eight-inch stainless steel skillet most frequently. It's great for searing, sautéing, and stir-frying. You can always add fat to the pan to prevent sticking, and it's difficult to properly sear in a nonstick skillet. I mainly use nonstick skillets for baking frittatas.

STAINLESS STEEL SAUTOIR. A sautoir is a flat-sided skillet. It's not a kitchen essential, but it's great for cooking risotto, skillet jams, and anything where there will be more liquid in the pan than a regular skillet can handle (for example, rendering fat from bacon or duck).

STAND MIXER. My stand mixer is a 4½-quart classic KitchenAid that has survived three generations. This thing is as sturdy as a rock. You really don't need larger, more expensive models for most recipes. I use my stand mixer for cakes, cookies, buttercreams, and kneading dough. It's a fantastic kitchen investment for bakers.

TART, QUICHE, AND PIE PANS. For tarts and quiches, I prefer to use shallow nonstick pans with removable bottoms. Wilton makes a great fluted pan that comes in a variety of sizes. When working with delicate dough such as pâte brisée (page 200), it's much easier to remove the tart when you can gently press up from the bottom. With regards to pie pans, pay close attention to whether a recipe calls for a standard or deep-dish pan.

WHISKS. I keep a few different-sized whisks in the kitchen and have recently become a fan of silicone whisks. You can press them right against the bottom of hot pans without scraping the surface.

HOMEMADE STOCKS

I always recommend using homemade stock; it's the foundation of good soups, sauces, and stews. Scale the ingredients up or down depending on the size of your stockpot. Don't worry about precise measurements and times. It doesn't have to be exact to yield results that are a million times better than anything purchased from the store.

It's important to cool chicken and seafood stock quickly to prevent bacteria from forming. To do this, place a large saucepan in the kitchen sink, surround it with ice, and strain the liquid through a fine mesh strainer lined with cheesecloth into the pot. Once the stock has cooled, transfer it to smaller containers and finish chilling in the refrigerator or freezer.

CHICKEN STOCK

PREP TIME: 30 minutes | **COOK TIME:** 8 hours (mostly inactive)
TOTAL TIME: 8 hours 30 minutes (mostly inactive) | **YIELD:** 2 to 3 quarts

Any type of raw chicken will work in stock. However, wings are a great choice because they contain a high level of collagen and are easily packed into a pot.

6 pounds raw chicken wings

2 medium yellow onions, quartered

2 medium carrots, quartered

2 ribs celery, quartered

1 cup packed fresh parsley

2 sprigs fresh thyme

1 to 2 bay leaves

3 whole black peppercorns

Approximately 1 gallon cold water

1. Place the wings, onions, carrots, celery, parsley, thyme, bay leaf, and peppercorns in a large stockpot. Fill the pot with cold water, covering the ingredients by 1 to 3 inches.

2. Bring the liquid to a gentle simmer over low heat (do not boil). Periodically skim the surface of the stock with a ladle, removing any bits of foam and scum that rise to the surface.

3. Simmer on the lowest possible setting for 6 to 8 hours, skimming periodically. Strain the liquid through a fine mesh strainer lined with cheesecloth, and discard the solids. Cool the stock over an ice bath (see page 14), then cover and refrigerate overnight.

4. Once chilled, use a spoon to remove and discard the congealed fat from the top of the stock.

Note: Chicken stock can be refrigerated for 3 to 4 days, frozen for several months, or pressure canned for up to 1 year.

VEGETABLE STOCK

PREP TIME: 30 minutes | **COOK TIME:** 1 hour 45 minutes (mostly inactive)
TOTAL TIME: 2 hours 15 minutes (mostly inactive) | **YIELD:** approximately 2 quarts

Roasting vegetables can add a tremendous amount of flavor to stock. To speed up the process, you can skip this step and combine the raw vegetables with cold water directly in the stockpot. Mushrooms can be used as a substitute for the strong savory flavor normally provided by chicken or seafood.

2 tablespoons extra-virgin olive oil

3 large yellow onions, quartered

2 large carrots, quartered

2 large leeks, washed thoroughly and quartered

2 ribs celery, quartered

6 to 8 ounces cremini or button mushrooms (optional)

Approximately 3 quarts cold water

4 to 5 sprigs fresh parsley

2 sprigs fresh thyme

1 bay leaf

2 to 3 whole black peppercorns

1. Preheat the oven to 400° F. Line a large baking sheet with aluminum foil.

2. In a large bowl, toss the oil with the onions, carrots, leeks, celery, and mushrooms, if using.

3. Spread the vegetables on the baking sheet and roast for 40 to 45 minutes, until lightly caramelized, stirring once midway through.

4. Place the vegetables in a large stockpot along with the parsley, thyme, bay leaf, and peppercorns. Add enough water to the pot to cover the ingredients by 1 to 3 inches. Bring the ingredients to a gentle simmer over low heat and cook for 1 hour. Strain the liquid through a fine mesh strainer lined with cheesecloth, discarding the solids.

Note: Vegetable stock can be refrigerated for 4 to 5 days, frozen for several months, or pressure canned for up to 1 year.

SEAFOOD STOCK

PREP TIME: 15 minutes | **COOK TIME:** 1 hour 30 minutes (mostly inactive)
TOTAL TIME: 1 hour 45 minutes (mostly inactive) | **YIELD:** 1½ to 2 quarts

Many seafood markets sell inexpensive, house-made stock. While it's cheaper to make your own, I don't use it regularly, so I typically purchase it to save time. When that's not an option, this is a great basic recipe to use in seafood-based soups, stews, and risottos. Seafood stock doesn't contain collagen, so it won't have a gelatinous quality like chicken stock. However, shrimp shells contain glutamates that will enhance the savory flavors in a recipe. Sometimes shrimp are sold with the heads attached; those can be added to this stock as well. The lobster and crab shells are optional, but will add flavor. You can freeze leftover shrimp, lobster, and crab shells from other recipes to use in stock.

Shells from 1½ to 2 pounds shrimp (5 to 7 cups)

Approximately 2 quarts cold water

Lobster and/or crab shells, broken into small pieces (optional)

1 medium yellow onion, chopped

1 medium carrot, chopped

1 rib celery, chopped

4 to 5 sprigs fresh parsley

1 sprig fresh thyme

3 to 4 whole black peppercorns

3 tablespoons tomato paste

⅓ cup dry white wine

1. Rinse and drain the shells. Preheat the oven to 400°F and line a large baking sheet with aluminum foil. Roast the shells for 10 to 15 minutes.

2. Place the shells in a large stockpot along with the onion, carrot, celery, parsley, thyme, and peppercorns. Add enough water to the pot to cover the ingredients by 1 to 3 inches. Turn the heat to medium. Once the mixture reaches a simmer, add the tomato paste and wine, and then reduce the heat to low. Simmer for 45 minutes to 1 hour, skimming the surface periodically with a ladle to remove any foam.

3. Strain the liquid through a fine mesh strainer lined with cheesecloth, and discard the solids. Cool the stock in an ice bath.

Note: Seafood stock can be refrigerated for 3 to 4 days, frozen for several months, or pressure canned for up to 1 year.

First we eat, then we do everything else.
—M. F. K. Fisher

BREAKFAST AND BRUNCH

When I was younger, I enjoyed sleeping in on the weekends and waking up to the smell of coffee, toast, and eggs. Once I was out of bed, Mom often prepared one of my favorite breakfasts, a "special" bagel. This was a toasted bagel with cream cheese that she'd place briefly under the broiler to caramelize the top of the cheese and get the underneath light and fluffy. I'd top each half with a healthy serving of strawberry preserves and enjoy it with orange juice. It was the best thing ever. These days, I'm more of a breakfast-for-dinner gal. I prefer something small and light to start my day, especially during the week. Something that will energize and fuel my body. Yogurt with granola or a frittata. However, that doesn't mean I don't have a deep appreciation for all things breakfast and brunch: muffins, scones, pancakes, cinnamon buns, and hearty breakfast sandwiches full of bacon and cheese. I love it all, just not first thing in the morning. But when it's time to get together with friends and family for a casual Sunday brunch, all bets are off. I'll take one of everything, please.

PARMESAN, ROSEMARY, AND THYME SCONES

PREP TIME: 13 minutes | **COOK TIME:** 12 minutes | **TOTAL TIME:** 25 minutes | **YIELD:** 12 scones

Fresh herbs can be a wonderful addition to both sweet and savory baked goods. Rosemary and thyme add a nice pop of earthiness and flavor to these buttery scones. As with any recipe that calls for Parmesan cheese, you should aim to use fresh Parmigiano-Reggiano cheese and grate it just before adding it to the dough. Real Parmesan cheese has a rich, nutty flavor that is markedly absent in pregrated cheese.

15 ounces (3 cups) all-purpose flour

1 tablespoon granulated sugar

2½ teaspoons baking powder

½ teaspoon baking soda

1 teaspoon kosher salt

½ cup plus ¼ cup freshly grated Parmigiano-Reggiano cheese

1½ teaspoons fresh rosemary, finely chopped

1½ teaspoons finely chopped fresh thyme leaves

6 ounces (12 tablespoons) unsalted butter, cold and cut into small pieces

1 cup buttermilk

2 tablespoons unsalted butter, melted, for brushing

1. Preheat the oven to 425°F. Line one large or two smaller baking sheets with parchment paper.

2. In a large bowl, whisk the flour, sugar, baking powder, baking soda, salt, ½ cup of the cheese, rosemary, and thyme.

3. Add the cold butter, and use your fingers or a pastry blender to work them into the dry ingredients until the mixture resembles coarse cornmeal with a few larger pieces here and there.

4. Add the buttermilk to the bowl and use a spatula to mix the ingredients until they are just combined. The dough will look like it's barely coming together. Knead the dough in the bowl until the dry ingredients are completely incorporated and the dough forms a smooth ball.

5. Divide the dough in half and flatten each half into two disks, approximately 7 inches in diameter. Cut each round into 6 wedges. Place the scones on the prepared baking sheets, brush the melted butter on top of each piece, and sprinkle generously with the remaining ¼ cup cheese.

6. Bake for 10 to 12 minutes, until both the tops and the bottoms are golden. Serve warm or at room temperature.

CARDAMOM VANILLA CREAM SCONES

PREP TIME: 15 minutes | **COOK TIME:** 12 minutes | **TOTAL TIME:** 27 minutes | **YIELD:** 12 scones

Cardamom and vanilla are both incredibly sweet and fragrant, and your kitchen will smell amazing while these scones are in the oven. I recommend serving them with your favorite tea. For best results, try to work the dough as little as possible. As with biscuits, a light touch leads to a flaky scone.

2 vanilla beans

15 ounces (3 cups) all-purpose flour

2 tablespoons granulated sugar

½ teaspoon ground cardamom

1 tablespoon baking powder

½ teaspoon baking soda

1 teaspoon kosher salt

6 ounces (12 tablespoons) unsalted butter, cold and cut into small pieces

1 cup light cream (half-and-half may be substituted)

1 teaspoon pure vanilla extract

2 tablespoons unsalted butter, melted

1. Preheat the oven to 425°F. Line one large or two smaller baking sheets with parchment paper.

2. Slice the vanilla beans in half lengthwise and use the flat side of a paring knife to scrape out the seeds.

3. In a medium bowl, whisk the flour, sugar, cardamom, baking powder, baking soda, and salt.

4. Add the cold butter pieces and, using your fingers or a pastry blender, work the butter into the dry ingredients until the mixture resembles coarse cornmeal with a few larger pieces scattered around.

5. Add the cream and vanilla to the bowl and use a spatula to mix the ingredients until they are just combined. Knead the dough in the bowl until it comes together. Divide the dough in half and flatten into two disks, approximately 7 inches in diameter. Cut each disk into 6 wedges. Brush the melted butter on top of each piece.

6. Bake for 10 to 12 minutes, until both the tops and the bottoms are golden. Serve warm.

SPINACH, ARTICHOKE, AND POTATO FRITTATA

PREP TIME: 15 minutes | **COOK TIME:** 10 minutes | **TOTAL TIME:** 25 minutes | **YIELD:** 8 to 10 servings

Frittatas have become a lifesaver for my husband, Jeff, and me. He likes taking breakfast with him to work and I'm often too rushed to prepare myself something during the week. While frittatas are definitely best when served fresh, they also make excellent leftovers. I will often prepare this on a Sunday and then divide it into individual portions that we can reheat throughout the week.

1 teaspoon kosher salt

¼ teaspoon ground black pepper

8 large eggs, beaten

1 (14½-ounce) can artichoke hearts, drained and coarsely chopped

1½ teaspoons extra-virgin olive oil

1 cup diced yellow onion, (approximately ½ medium)

1 medium russet potato, peeled and diced

1 clove garlic, minced

3 cups packed fresh spinach, coarsely chopped

½ cup crumbled feta cheese

1. Preheat the oven to 400°F.

2. In a small bowl, whisk the salt and pepper into the eggs and set aside. Gently pat the artichokes with paper towels to remove excess moisture.

3. Heat the oil in a 10- or 12-inch oven-safe nonstick skillet over medium-low heat. Add the onion and cook for 1 to 2 minutes, until translucent. Add the potato, increase the heat to medium, and sauté, stirring periodically, until the potato is slightly caramelized and cooked through. This will take anywhere from 5 to 10 minutes.

4. Stir in the garlic and cook for another minute until fragrant. Add the spinach and stir. Once the spinach is almost completely wilted, add the artichokes.

5. Use the back of a spatula to gently press the ingredients flat into the skillet. Sprinkle the crumbled feta evenly on top. Briefly rewhisk the eggs to redistribute the salt and pepper, and then slowly pour evenly over the cheese and vegetables.

6. Place the skillet into the oven and bake for 10 to 12 minutes or until the top has set (it should not jiggle).

7. Allow to cool briefly before slicing and serving.

TOASTED COCONUT BARS

While I appreciate the idea behind store-bought fruit-and-nut bars, they're almost always too sweet for me. These toasted coconut bars are easy to make at home and have a balanced flavor. Medjool dates have a neutral sweetness and make a wonderful binder. Toasted coconut is the primary flavor, enhanced by heart-healthy coconut oil as well as coconut butter, which I consider to be the secret ingredient. If you can't find coconut butter, it can be replaced with additional coconut oil. Add the extra oil 1 tablespoon at a time, until the mixture holds when pressed together.

1 tablespoon coconut oil, plus more for pan

⅔ cup unsweetened shredded coconut

2 cups unsalted cashews

1 cup Medjool dates, pitted

⅛ teaspoon kosher salt

¼ teaspoon ground cinnamon

¼ cup plus 2 tablespoons coconut butter

1. Preheat the oven to 350°F. Line an 8 x 8-inch pan with parchment paper, allowing two sides to hang over the side of the pan. Spread a bit of coconut oil in the pan to help the parchment paper stick to the two sides. Set aside.

2. Spread the coconut in a thin layer on a baking sheet and toast in the oven for 2 to 3 minutes. Stir well and then toast for another 2 to 3 minutes, or until fragrant and golden.

3. Remove the coconut from the oven and set aside. Use the same baking sheet to toast the cashews for 4 to 6 minutes, or until fragrant.

4. Add the toasted coconut, cashews, dates, salt, and cinnamon to a food processor.

5. Pulse the ingredients several times until they're crumb size. Add the 1 tablespoon coconut oil and the coconut butter to the food processor, and pulse until the mixture begins to clump together.

6. Press the mixture into the pan, using plastic wrap or a kitchen glove to help flatten as evenly as possible. Freeze the pan for 20 minutes and then slice into 8 bars.

7. Wrap the toasted coconut bars individually and store in the refrigerator or freezer.

SOUTHWESTERN AVOCADO TOAST

PREP TIME: 7 minutes | **COOK TIME:** 3 minutes | **TOTAL TIME:** 10 minutes | **YIELD:** 4 toasts

I'm not going to pretend this avocado toast isn't basically guacamole toast; it is. But I am a guacamole fanatic, and if having guacamole toast for breakfast is wrong, I don't want to be right. Black beans add some hearty protein, and queso fresco adds a bit of luxury. Queso fresco ("fresh cheese") is a Mexican cheese that has a milky, mild flavor and a firm texture that is easily crumbled. Feel free to add more or less of each topping to taste, and if you're not a fan of heat, skip the peppers.

4 slices crusty artisan bread

2 ripe avocados, peeled and pitted

2 tablespoons fresh-squeezed lime juice (approximately 1 lime)

Kosher salt

1 cup cooked black beans

4 teaspoons finely diced shallot (red onion may be substituted)

1 to 2 jalapeño or serrano peppers, seeded and finely diced

2 tablespoons crumbled queso fresco

4 teaspoons chopped fresh cilantro

1. Toast the bread and place the slices onto four separate plates.

2. In a small bowl, mash the avocados, lime juice, and a pinch of salt. Spread evenly on each of the 4 slices of toast.

3. Top each toast with ¼ cup of the black beans, 1 teaspoon of the shallot, a sprinkle of diced pepper, ½ tablespoon of the queso fresco, 1 teaspoon of the cilantro, and a sprinkle of salt.

4. Serve immediately.

ITALIAN BAKED EGGS

PREP TIME: 5 minutes | **COOK TIME:** 15 minutes | **TOTAL TIME:** 20 minutes | **YIELD:** 4 baked eggs

These baked eggs make a wonderful addition to any brunch menu. The recipe can be easily scaled up or down depending on how many people are being served. If I'm serving guests, I'll prepare the ramekins before company arrives so all I have to do is pop the baking sheet in the oven. The ramekins will be very hot (scoop the baked eggs into a cool bowl if you're serving children).

4 teaspoons good quality extra-virgin olive oil

8 to 10 grape tomatoes, sliced into thirds

4 teaspoons fresh basil, sliced thin

4 large eggs

4 teaspoons freshly grated Parmigiano-Reggiano cheese

¼ teaspoon kosher salt

¼ teaspoon ground black pepper

1. Preheat the oven to 350°F.

2. Prepare four 4- or 6-ounce ramekins by adding 1 teaspoon oil to each. Use clean hands or a pastry brush to grease the sides of the ramekins with the oil.

3. Layer 4 to 6 slices of tomatoes on the bottom of each ramekin (this will create a bed for the eggs).

4. Sprinkle 1 teaspoon of the basil into each ramekin.

5. Crack 1 egg into each ramekin (to make sure no shells are accidentally added, crack each egg into a separate container first).

6. Top each egg with 1 teaspoon of the cheese followed by a sprinkle of salt and pepper to taste.

7. Place the ramekins on a baking sheet and then place the sheet in the oven. Bake for 15 minutes, or until the whites are set but the yolks are still runny. Serve immediately.

BROWN BUTTER NECTARINE MUFFINS

PREP TIME: 15 minutes | COOK TIME: 25 minutes | TOTAL TIME: 40 minutes | YIELD: 12 muffins

Despite popular misconception, brown butter is easy to prepare. The key is to constantly whisk the butter once it has melted and begins to foam, to prevent burning. If prepared with care, the butter will develop a golden-brown color and a rich, nutty flavor. If browning butter still feels too far outside of your comfort zone, don't worry; normal melted butter will work just as well in these muffins. They will still taste wonderful.

4 ounces (8 tablespoons) unsalted butter, cut into small pieces

7½ ounces (1½ cups) all-purpose flour

½ cup granulated sugar

2 tablespoons cornstarch

2 teaspoons baking powder

½ teaspoon ground cinnamon

2 ripe, unpeeled nectarines, finely diced

1 large egg

1 teaspoon pure vanilla extract

¾ cup 2% milk (or milk of your choice)

Approximately 1 tablespoon light brown sugar

1. Preheat the oven to 350°F. Line a 12-cup muffin pan with paper baking cups, or lightly grease each muffin round, using baking spray or butter.

2. To prepare the brown butter, melt the butter in a medium saucepan over medium heat. As the butter melts, whisk frequently until foam begins to appear. Once it begins to foam, whisk constantly until the butter begins to brown and it smells nutty and fragrant. Remove from the heat and allow to cool (see note).

3. In a large bowl, whisk the flour, granulated sugar, cornstarch, baking powder, and cinnamon. Stir in the nectarines and make sure the pieces don't clump together.

4. In a separate medium bowl, whisk the egg, vanilla, milk, and brown butter. Stir the wet ingredients into the dry until just combined. Don't overwork the batter; some lumps are fine.

5. Scoop the batter evenly into the pan and sprinkle a bit of brown sugar on top of each muffin.

6. Bake for 22 to 25 minutes, or until a toothpick inserted into the center of a muffin comes out clean. Allow to cool for 5 minutes.

7. Enjoy warm or at room temperature.

Note: Butter can go from brown to burned very quickly; do not leave it unattended.

HONEY THYME CRÈME FRAÎCHE MUFFINS

PREP TIME: 10 minutes | **COOK TIME:** 20 minutes | **TOTAL TIME:** 30 minutes | **YIELD:** 12 muffins

I've become such a big fan of crème fraîche. It's a fancier version of sour cream, so if your grocery store doesn't carry it, sour cream will get the job done (or you can make your own; see page 7). Crème fraîche does have a milder flavor and is less sour. It has a rich and creamy mouthfeel that makes these muffins really wonderful. I recommend using a mild-flavored olive oil (and if you're not sure, taste the oil before adding it to the recipe). Go for a fruity oil instead of one that's overly grassy or peppery. A mild olive oil will enhance the delicate, earthy flavors of thyme and honey; a strong oil will easily overpower those flavors.

Baking spray

10½ ounces (2¼ cups) all-purpose flour

1 tablespoon baking powder

¼ teaspoon kosher salt

1 teaspoon chopped fresh thyme leaves

¼ cup extra-virgin olive oil

½ cup crème fraîche

¼ cup honey

1 cup skim milk

1. Preheat the oven to 350°F. Line a 12-cup muffin pan with paper baking cups and lightly spray them with baking spray (you can omit the liners if you prefer, but still grease the pan).

2. In a large bowl, whisk the flour, baking powder, salt, and thyme. In a separate bowl, whisk the oil, crème fraîche, honey, and milk.

3. Pour the liquid ingredients into the dry ingredients and stir until just combined.

4. Scoop the batter evenly among the liners and bake for 20 to 25 minutes, or until a toothpick inserted into the center of a muffin comes out clean. Allow to cool for at least 5 minutes.

5. Serve warm or at room temperature.

BAKED EGGNOG FRENCH TOAST

PREP TIME: 45 minutes (mostly inactive) | **COOK TIME:** 55 minutes | **TOTAL TIME:** 1 hour 40 minutes (mostly inactive) | **YIELD:** 8 servings

Shopping for eggnog is a bit like shopping for wine; you can't buy just anything and expect it to taste good. Organic Valley makes superior eggnog, as does Southern Comfort. Avoid generic brands and low-fat varieties for optimal flavor. In addition to being a tasty holiday drink, eggnog makes the most decadent French toast you can imagine. For this recipe, you can do most of the prep work in the evening, and then simply bake come morning.

2 cups good-quality eggnog

1 large egg

1½ teaspoons pure vanilla extract

1 tablespoon unsalted butter, softened

9 to 10 cups day-old challah (approximately one loaf), chopped into 1-inch cubes

1¼ ounces (¼ cup) all-purpose flour

¼ cup packed light brown sugar

⅛ teaspoon kosher salt

3 tablespoons unsalted butter, cold and cut into small pieces

1. In a medium bowl, whisk the eggnog, egg, and vanilla.

2. Grease a 9 x 5-inch loaf pan with the butter and layer the challah inside the pan, gently pressing it flat. Briefly rewhisk the liquid ingredients and pour them evenly over the bread, taking care to cover all the exposed bread. Cover with plastic wrap and refrigerate for a minimum of 30 minutes or as long as overnight to allow the bread to absorb the mixture.

3. When ready to bake, preheat the oven to 350°F. In a small bowl, use a fork to combine the flour, sugar, salt, and butter until the mixture looks crumbly.

4. Uncover the loaf pan and gently press the bread down evenly until the liquid begins seeping up over the bread. Spread the topping evenly over the bread. Bake for 50 to 55 minutes, until the top is golden and crunchy.

5. Allow to cool for several minutes and then slice and serve.

OLD BAY POTATO LATKES

PREP TIME: 20 minutes | **COOK TIME:** 15 minutes | **TOTAL TIME:** 35 minutes | **YIELD:** 10 to 13 latkes

We use a lot of Old Bay in Maryland, my home state. It's a spice mainly associated with seafood, but I think it works well in a wide range of recipes. The flavor reminds me of my childhood, and this latke recipe just says "home" to me. Old Bay includes quite a bit of salt, so you want to use it somewhat sparingly. To make sure the flavor was noticeable without oversalting the latkes, I added some of the individual spices used in Old Bay, including sweet paprika and celery seed.

2 large russet potatoes, peeled and cubed

½ cup finely diced yellow onion (approximately ½ medium)

½ medium clove (or 1 small clove) garlic, minced

1 large egg

½ cup diced poblano pepper (green peppers may be substituted)

1½ tablespoons all-purpose flour

2 teaspoons Old Bay seasoning

⅛ teaspoon ground black pepper

½ teaspoon celery seed

¼ teaspoon sweet paprika

⅛ teaspoon ground mustard

Vegetable oil

Sour cream or applesauce for serving

1. In a food processor fitted with a metal blade, pulse the potatoes 3 to 4 times. Add the onion, garlic, egg, and poblano pepper, and pulse several more times to incorporate the ingredients. Add the flour, Old Bay, black pepper, celery seed, paprika, and mustard. Puree until just smooth and fluffy (the mixture should still retain some texture). Do not overmix. Transfer the mixture to a fine mesh strainer and allow a portion of the water to drain for 5 minutes.

2. Generously coat the bottom of a large nonstick skillet with vegetable oil (use 2 to 3 tablespoons for a 12-inch skillet). Set over medium-high heat. When the oil is shimmering, use a ¼-cup measure to portion out the mixture into the pan, making sure the latkes don't touch each other. Flatten slightly with the back of the measuring cup or a spatula. Cook in batches to avoid overcrowding the pan and be careful to avoid oil splatters.

3. Fry the latkes until golden brown, 2 to 3 minutes per side, adding fresh oil to the pan between batches as needed.

4. Transfer the latkes to a paper towel–lined baking sheet to drain. Serve immediately with sour cream or applesauce.

BLUEBERRY CASHEW GRANOLA

PREP TIME: 15 minutes | **COOK TIME:** 1 hour | **TOTAL TIME:** 1 hour 15 minutes
YIELD: Approximately 6½ cups

This blueberry cashew granola is one of my favorite breakfasts. Mix in some fresh, tart blueberries and plain, tangy yogurt, and you'll have a perfectly balanced, filling breakfast that doesn't skimp on flavor or nutrition. If you're unable to find dried blueberries, feel free to substitute your favorite dried fruit.

2½ cups old-fashioned rolled oats

1½ cups raw cashews, coarsely chopped

½ teaspoon kosher salt

2 teaspoons ground cinnamon

¾ cup pure maple syrup

1 teaspoon pure vanilla extract

1 cup dried blueberries

Fresh blueberries and plain yogurt or milk (optional)

1. Preheat the oven to 225°F. Line a large baking sheet with parchment paper.

2. In a large bowl, combine the oats, cashews, salt, and cinnamon. In a liquid measuring cup, stir the maple syrup and vanilla extract. Pour the liquid ingredients over the dry ingredients and stir until evenly combined.

3. Spread the mixture in a thin layer across the parchment paper. Bake the granola for 1 hour.

4. Remove from the oven and allow to cool. Toss with the dried blueberries.

5. Serve the granola with fresh blueberries and yogurt or milk, if using.

Note: The granola can be stored in an airtight container for up to 2 weeks at room temperature.

APPLE, SWEET POTATO, AND BACON TURNOVERS

PREP TIME: 1 hour 10 minutes | **COOK TIME:** 25 minutes | **TOTAL TIME:** 1 hour 35 minutes
YIELD: 12 turnovers

When I was in culinary school, we always made puff pastry from scratch. While the home-made stuff is certainly outstanding, I never bother with it anymore. Store-bought frozen puff pastry works perfectly and saves so much time. The key is to keep the dough chilled until just before working with it. If your dough gets too soft and buttery while working on these turnovers, place it back in the refrigerator for at least fifteen minutes to firm up. These turnovers are worth the wait. They have a wonderful balance of sweet and salty that makes them a fun treat for breakfast or brunch. They also make a great party appetizer.

1 medium sweet potato (approximately 8 ounces), peeled and diced

2 slices good-quality bacon, diced

1 large tart apple (such as Granny Smith), peeled, cored, and coarsely chopped

2 tablespoons unsalted butter

¼ teaspoon freshly ground nutmeg

½ teaspoon ground cinnamon, divided

1½ teaspoons pure maple syrup

Kosher salt

All-purpose flour for dusting

3 sheets puff pastry, chilled

1 large egg

1. Boil a large pot of water and cook the sweet potato until soft, approximately 10 minutes (the smaller the dice, the faster it will cook). Drain and set aside.

2. In a large skillet, cook the bacon over low heat for several minutes to render the fat. Then turn the heat to medium and cook for several more minutes, until caramelized and crisp. Allow the bacon to drain well on a paper towel.

3. In a Dutch oven or heavy-bottom saucepan, melt the butter over medium-low heat and add the apple. Toss to coat the apple and then add the nutmeg and ¼ teaspoon of the cinnamon. Cook the apple, stirring frequently, until lightly caramelized and softer but not mushy. Set aside.

4. Mash the sweet potato and stir in the maple syrup, the remaining ¼ teaspoon cinnamon, and a pinch of salt. Set aside.

5. Line 2 baking sheets with parchment paper and preheat the oven to 400°F.

6. Lightly dust a clean surface with flour and roll out one chilled sheet of puff pastry to approximately 12 x 12 inches (keep the other sheets in the refrigerator until the last sec-

recipe continued on next page

ond). You will want to work swiftly with the dough before it becomes too soft. Square off the dough if necessary with a bench scraper or pizza cutter and slice into four 6-inch squares.

7. Place 1 tablespoon of the sweet potato mixture inside one of the squares. Top with 1½ tablespoons of apple and 1 heaping teaspoon of chopped bacon. Make sure to leave some space between the filling and the sides of the dough so that the turnover can be sealed once it's folded. Repeat this process with the remaining 3 pieces of dough.

8. Fold the dough over from corner to corner into a triangle shape. Use a fork to press the edges together firmly and seal in the filling.

9. Place the turnovers on a baking sheet and place in the refrigerator for at least 15 minutes.

10. Repeat the same process with the remaining sheets of puff pastry and the remainder of the filling, placing the turnovers onto the second prepared baking sheet (divide evenly so there are 6 turnovers per baking sheet).

11. In a small bowl, whisk the egg with a splash of water and a pinch of salt.

12. Remove the baking sheets from the refrigerator and use a small knife to poke 3 holes in the top of each turnover. Use a pastry brush to spread a thin layer of egg wash over each turnover.

13. Bake for 20 to 25 minutes, or until the dough is cooked through and golden brown on top.

ORANGE CARDAMOM CINNAMON BUNS

PREP TIME: 3 hours (mostly inactive) | **COOK TIME:** 30 minutes
TOTAL TIME: 3 hours 30 minutes (mostly inactive) | **YIELD:** 12 to 16 buns

Cardamom is most often encountered in Indian cuisine and Scandinavian baking, but I often use it in a variety of dishes, especially baked goods and desserts. It has a sweet, exotic flavor that pairs amazingly well with sugar, citrus, and other spices. These orange cardamom cinnamon buns are always a hit when I serve them at brunch gatherings. They're soft, fluffy, and have just the right level of sweetness.

FOR THE DOUGH:

½ cup whole milk, warmed
(110° to 115°F)

2¼ teaspoons instant yeast

3 large eggs

20 ounces (4 cups) all-purpose flour, plus
¼ cup if needed

3¼ ounces (¾ cup) cornstarch

½ cup granulated sugar

1 teaspoon kosher salt

⅛ teaspoon ground cardamom

1½ teaspoons grated orange zest

¼ cup fresh-squeezed orange juice
(approximately 1 orange)

6 ounces (12 tablespoons) unsalted
butter, cut into small pieces and at room
temperature

FOR THE FILLING:

1½ cups packed light brown sugar

1 tablespoon ground cinnamon

1¼ teaspoons ground cardamom

¼ teaspoon kosher salt

2 ounces (4 tablespoons) unsalted butter,
room temperature

FOR THE GLAZE:

7½ ounces (1½ cups) confectioners' sugar

4 ounces cream cheese, room temperature

¼ cup fresh-squeezed orange juice
(approximately 1 medium orange)

½ teaspoon pure vanilla extract

1. To make the dough, in a large liquid measuring cup, whisk the milk and yeast, followed by the eggs.

2. In the bowl of a stand mixer, whisk the flour, cornstarch, granulated sugar, salt, ⅛ teaspoon cardamom, and orange zest. Break apart any clumps of zest if necessary. Attach the dough hook, turn the mixer on low speed, and add the warm milk mixture followed by the orange

recipe continued on next page

juice. Allow the ingredients to combine for 1 minute. Increase the speed to medium and add the butter in pieces until it's all incorporated—at this stage, the dough will be very wet. Allow it to continue mixing for 10 more minutes. If the dough is still wet, add up to another ¼ cup of flour in 2-tablespoon increments until incorporated. When finished, the dough should be very soft and delicate but not too sticky to handle. Transfer the dough to a lightly greased large bowl and cover with a clean kitchen towel. Allow the dough to double in size, up to 2 hours at room temperature. To speed things up, you can place the bowl inside the oven or microwave next to a small bowl of boiling water and close the door.

3. To prepare the filling, while the dough is rising, combine the brown sugar, cinnamon, 1¼ teaspoons cardamom, and the salt in a small bowl. Grease two 8-inch cake pans thoroughly using baking spray or butter and set aside.

4. Place the dough on a lightly floured countertop. Roll the dough into a large, thin rectangle (suggested 19 x 14 inches). Using clean hands, spread the butter across the dough, leaving a small unbuttered border around the edges, and then top evenly with the sugar mixture. Roll the dough into a tight cylinder. Cut into 12 to 16 even pieces and place in the reserved cake pans, cut side up. Cover and allow the dough to double in size at room temperature, approximately 1 hour.

5. To prepare the glaze, whisk the confectioners' sugar, cream cheese, orange juice, and vanilla. Set aside.

6. Bake the buns at 350°F for 30 to 35 minutes, or until the tops are golden brown. Top each cake pan with ¼ cup of the glaze and allow the buns to cool completely. Top with the remaining glaze just before serving.

SWEET POTATO AND BACON HASH WITH EGGS

PREP TIME: 10 minutes | **COOK TIME:** 35 minutes | **TOTAL TIME:** 45 minutes | **YIELD:** 4 servings

This is a perfect breakfast for those mornings when I'm looking for a high protein meal that will give me a lot of energy for the day. It's brain and body food that will get me through workouts, long meetings, or an extended food photography shoot. It has a lot of textural elements to balance the delicate eggs, and I love the way the salty bacon pairs with sweet potatoes. This is a hearty, satisfying meal—it also works well for dinner.

3 slices thick-cut bacon

3 medium sweet potatoes, peeled and diced (4 to 5 cups)

1 cup diced yellow onion (approximately ½ medium)

1 cup Brussels sprouts, sliced thin

¼ teaspoon kosher salt

Ground black pepper

4 large eggs

1. Preheat the oven to 375°F. Line a baking sheet with aluminum foil.

2. Cook the bacon in a large sauté pan over medium-low heat until crisp, rendering the fat. Use tongs to transfer the bacon to a paper towel–lined plate. After the bacon has cooled, dice and set aside.

3. Save approximately 1 tablespoon of bacon fat to toss with the sweet potatoes (alternately, 1 to 2 tablespoons olive oil may be used in place of the bacon fat). Once tossed, spread on the baking sheet and roast in the oven until soft, approximately 30 minutes, stirring halfway through to prevent sticking.

4. While the sweet potatoes are cooking, sauté the onion and Brussels sprouts over medium heat until tender and slightly caramelized, 10 to 15 minutes.

5. In a large bowl, toss the sweet potatoes, bacon, and onion, Brussels sprouts, salt, and pepper.

6. Cook the eggs according to preference (poached or fried eggs work well with this recipe).

7. Serve the eggs over the hash.

SPICED PLUM BUTTER

PREP TIME: 10 minutes | **COOK TIME:** 1 hour 20 minutes | **TOTAL TIME:** 1 hour 30 minutes
YIELD: 3 to 4 cups

I have control issues around homemade jams and butters; I eat them straight from the jar with a spoon. This plum butter is dangerous like that. The final product has a beautiful color, a sweet and tangy flavor, and a rich fragrance. It's really good served on fresh crusty bread with a bit of ricotta cheese. The ripeness of the plums used in this recipe will have a dramatic effect on the flavor. Firmer, less ripe plums are typically more tart, while soft, ripe plums are sweeter. For a nice flavor balance, use a mixture of both ripe and semiripe plums. If you use all ripe plums, you might want to use less honey (and possibly a tablespoon or two of fresh-squeezed lemon juice for tartness). If your plums are very tart to begin with, add more honey to taste.

4 to 4½ pounds ripe and semiripe plums, pitted

1 orange or 2 clementines, unpeeled

½ teaspoon pure vanilla extract

½ teaspoon ground cinnamon

¼ teaspoon ground allspice

½ cup honey

1. In a blender or food processor, puree the plums. If they are firm, chop them up first.

2. Push the plum puree through a food mill and discard the skins (see note). Pour the puree into a Dutch oven or heavy-bottom saucepan.

3. Use a vegetable peeler to peel 4 large strips of zest from the orange. Juice the fruit, and add 3 tablespoons of juice to the Dutch oven along with the zest. Stir in the vanilla, cinnamon, allspice, and honey.

4. Bring the mixture to a boil, stirring periodically, then reduce the heat to low. Simmer for 75 to 80 minutes, uncovered, and use tongs to remove the zest after 20 minutes. Stir frequently, scraping a heatproof spatula against the bottom of the pan to make sure nothing sticks.

5. Allow to cool.

Notes: If you do not have a food mill, you can remove the skins by blanching the whole plums in boiling water for 15 to 30 seconds before removing skins and pureeing.

Store in an airtight container in the refrigerator for up to 1 month.

CHERRY VANILLA BEAN JAM

PREP TIME: 30 minutes | **COOK TIME:** 45 minutes | **TOTAL TIME:** 1 hour 15 minutes | **YIELD:** 5 to 6 cups

If you've never made homemade jam but have always wanted to try, the skillet is a great way to go. Skillet jams come together quickly and don't involve much prep work, aside from the cherry pitting in this instance (do yourself a favor and use a cherry pitter, if you can). Also, be sure to wear kitchen gloves and an apron. I speak from experience! This jam is wonderful by itself (with a spoon), served on toast, or used as an ingredient in my Cherry Vanilla Jam Crumb Bars (page 250).

6 cups (approximately 3 pounds) cherries, pitted and coarsely chopped

3 cups granulated sugar

2 vanilla beans, split and scraped

½ tablespoon fresh-squeezed lemon juice

1. Add the cherries, sugar, and vanilla seed scrapings to a large, flat-sided skillet or Dutch oven (discard the vanilla bean pods or save for another use). Stir and allow the mixture to macerate for at least 15 minutes, to allow some liquid to release from the cherries.

2. Turn the heat to medium and allow the liquid to come to a simmer while stirring periodically. Stir in the lemon juice.

3. The skillet will continue to fill with liquid as it is released from the cherries. Continue stirring the jam frequently as it simmers, until most of the liquid has evaporated or thickened, 30 to 45 minutes. Remember that the jam will continue to thicken once it cools.

4. Once the jam has thickened enough that you can drag a spatula through it without the jam quickly rushing to fill the space, remove the skillet from the heat.

Note: To test if the jam has properly gelled, you can place a small plate in the freezer before getting started. When you suspect that the jam is ready, place a very small spoonful on the chilled plate and return it to the freezer. After 3 to 4 minutes, check to see if the jam has gelled. With a bit of practice, you'll be able to tell if the jam is ready just from looking at it. You can freeze this in an airtight container for 3 months, or store in the refrigerator for up to 1 month.

ORANGE GRAND MARNIER SKILLET JAM

PREP TIME: 20 minutes | **COOK TIME:** 40 minutes | **TOTAL TIME:** 1 hour | **YIELD:** approximately 2 cups

I'm not sure if everyone will like the idea of adding liqueur to fruit jam. It's not something that I frequently do, but Grand Marnier is one of my favorite liqueurs because it really enhances the flavor of oranges (and strawberries, as you'll see in the recipe for Strawberry Grand Marnier Mini Layer Cake, page 240). It certainly can be omitted if you'd prefer an alcohol-free version. This recipe is reminiscent of marmalade, but it's much easier to prepare.

6 oranges, peeled, seeded, and segmented (approximately 6 cups)

2 teaspoons grated orange zest

2 cups granulated sugar

¼ cup Grand Marnier

2 tablespoons fresh-squeezed lemon juice (approximately 1 lemon)

1. Slice the orange segments crosswise in half. While you don't necessarily *have* to do this step, it will help the oranges break down faster while the jam is cooking.

2. Add the orange segments, zest, and sugar to a large skillet and stir. Allow the unheated mixture to sit at room temperature for 15 minutes, stirring a few times. Add the Grand Marnier and lemon juice.

3. Place the skillet over medium heat. As the oranges heat and begin to simmer they will release a lot of liquid. Continue cooking for 35 to 40 minutes, stirring periodically. As the liquid begins to reduce and thicken, stir more frequently to avoid burning the jam.

4. Once the oranges are completely broken down and the remaining liquid has thickened into a syrup, remove from the heat. Allow to cool.

Note: Store in an airtight container in the refrigerator for up to 1 month, or in the freezer for up to 3 months.

SOUPS AND SALADS

It wasn't until I learned to cook that I began to fully appreciate soups and salads, but I had no idea how to prepare either from scratch. Now that I've gotten the hang of it, homemade soups and salads are a staple of my diet. They are the epitome of comfort food. Some of these recipes are absolutely suitable as a main course. You won't find a more perfect winter meal than my salmon soup with udon and mushrooms, while my hearty steak salad with tahini vinaigrette is filling and flavorful year-round.

When it comes to homemade soup, patience is key. You want to allow flavors to slowly build through caramelization of vegetables, allowing a brown glaze to form on the bottom of the pan, and then using liquid to "deglaze" the brown bits. Aromatics, such as onions and garlic, should almost always be included, and a splash of wine or brandy while deglazing is a quick way to add a ton of flavor. Homemade stock makes a major difference in the final outcome, so I highly recommend making your own (see chapter Homemade Stocks, page 14) It is also sometimes available from local butchers, seafood markets, and gourmet shops. A Dutch oven or heavy-bottom saucepan is an important tool, and a sturdy, powerful blender, while not essential, will improve the overall texture.

Good salads are all about creating a balance of flavors, textures, colors, and a bit of fat to enhance the lighter ingredients. My favorite salads take advantage of all four tastes: sweet, bitter, sour, and salty. I love using fresh and dried fruits, candied nuts, or balsamic vinegar for sweetness. Arugula or radishes are a great source of bitterness. Lemon juice or fresh cranberries are examples of ways to add that sour note. Use a good salty cheese such as Roquefort or feta (or a crunchy, coarse salt). Toss everything with a properly balanced vinaigrette. For texture, add some nuts or crunchy vegetables. Fat comes in many wonderful forms such as cheese, a good-quality olive oil, or avocados.

SOUPS

CREAM OF SHIITAKE MUSHROOM AND CARAMELIZED LEEK SOUP

PREP TIME: 15 minutes | **COOK TIME:** 1 hour 15 minutes | **TOTAL TIME:** 1 hour 30 minutes | **YIELD:** 4 to 6 servings

The first time I cooked with leeks, I had no idea what to do with them. I was preparing a pumpkin risotto and the recipe didn't specify to avoid the dark green fibrous tops, so I used the entire leek. Over time I learned that while the tops add flavor to stock, the best part of the leek is the pale green and white section. It's important to wash leeks very thoroughly. The best way to do this is to slice each leek in half lengthwise. Fan open each half and place under cold running water, rinsing out any dirt or sand. Leeks have a delicate onion flavor and they also caramelize beautifully. They pair well with mushrooms and cream for a rich and hearty soup. The flavors in this soup are much more intense and pronounced the next day, so if there is time, I recommend preparing it a day in advance. The white truffle oil is an optional ingredient, but a tiny amount of it adds a depth and earthiness to the soup without overwhelming the other flavors.

1 tablespoon unsalted butter

2 cups leeks, white and pale green parts only, thinly sliced (approximately 2 leeks)

Pinch of kosher salt

5 cups shiitake mushrooms (tough stems removed), roughly chopped

3 cloves garlic, smashed

½ cup dry white wine

4 cups chicken or vegetable stock, preferably homemade (pages 15 and 16)

½ cup heavy cream, plus more as needed

1¼ teaspoon kosher salt, plus more as needed

Ground black pepper

¼ teaspoon good-quality white truffle oil (optional)

1. Heat the butter in a large Dutch oven over low heat. Keep a small cup of water nearby. Add the leeks with a pinch of salt and stir to coat with the butter. Allow the leeks to sweat for 2 to 3 minutes and then turn up the heat to medium-low. Allow the leeks to slowly caramelize, stirring frequently, 15 to 20 minutes. As a brown glaze forms on the bottom of the pan, add 1 to 2 tablespoons of water at a time and stir to incorporate the glaze back into the leeks. Once they are nicely caramelized, approximately 10 minutes, add the mushrooms.

recipe continued on next page

2. Continue to cook the mushrooms and leeks for another 3 to 5 minutes, stirring frequently and deglazing with water as needed, until the mushrooms have softened and shrunk down a bit in size. Add the garlic and stir for another 30 seconds. Deglaze with the wine, scraping up the brown bits that will have formed on the bottom of the pot and incorporating them into the vegetables.

3. Allow the wine to reduce to almost nothing and then add the stock. Bring the soup to a boil, cover the pot, and reduce the heat to low. Allow the soup to simmer for 1 hour.

4. Ladle the soup into a blender and puree, in batches if necessary, until silky smooth. Pour the soup back into the pan and add the cream, salt, and pepper. Add the truffle oil, if using. If a thinner consistency is desired, add more cream.

5. Ladle into small bowls and serve hot.

ANDOUILLE CORN CHOWDER

PREP TIME: 15 minutes | **COOK TIME:** 40 minutes | **TOTAL TIME:** 55 minutes | **YIELD:** 5 to 6 servings

I consider corn to be primarily a summer vegetable, but this is one of those recipes that can be enjoyed year-round. There aren't many hot soups I want to eat when it's warm and humid outside, but I will always make an exception for corn chowder, especially this version with Andouille sausage. If fresh corn isn't available, frozen corn may be substituted. There's no need to thaw it out, simply add it directly to the chowder in step five. Since corn chowder is already very rich, I recommend using precooked turkey Andouille sausage in this recipe. It has less fat than pork Andouille and the flavors are less likely to overpower the delicate corn flavor.

1 tablespoon clarified butter or extra-virgin olive oil

9 ounces (approximately 3 links) precooked turkey Andouille sausage, diced small

1½ cups diced yellow onion (approximately 1 large)

½ teaspoon kosher salt, plus a pinch

2 tablespoons all-purpose flour

1 large or 2 small cloves garlic, minced

2½ cups chicken stock, preferably homemade (page 15)

1 medium russet potato

1½ cups whole milk or half-and-half

Kernels from 4 medium ears of corn (approximately 3 cups)

Ground black pepper

1 tablespoon unsalted butter to finish (optional)

Chopped fresh parsley for garnish

1. Heat the butter in a large Dutch oven or heavy-bottom saucepan. Brown the sausage over medium-low heat until crisp. Remove from the pan and set aside.

2. Add the onion and a pinch of salt to the Dutch oven. Place a liquid measuring cup filled with water near the stove. Allow the onion to cook for several minutes, stirring periodically as it begins to caramelize. A brown glaze will begin forming on the bottom of the pan. If at any point the bottom of the pan looks like it's about to become too dark and start burning, add 1 to 2 tablespoons of the reserved water and scrape the brown bits back into the onion. Once the onion is soft and lightly caramelized, add the flour, tossing it with the onion to coat. Add the garlic and cook for another minute.

3. A brown coating should begin to form on the bottom of the pan, this time from the flour. Once the pan has a brown glaze, add the chicken stock and use a spatula to scrape the brown bits up from the bottom of the pan so they combine with the liquid. Bring the mixture to a boil over high heat.

4. While the stock is heating, peel and dice the potato

recipe continued on next page

(a small or medium dice). Once the stock is boiling, add the milk along with the diced potato. Turn the heat to medium-low and allow the mixture to simmer for 15 minutes, uncovered, stirring frequently to prevent the potatoes from sticking to the bottom of the pan.

5. Add the corn kernels and simmer for another 8 to 9 minutes, stirring frequently. Add the sausage, salt, and pepper and stir for another 1 to 2 minutes.

6. If using butter to finish, stir just after removing the pan from the heat. Top each serving with fresh chopped parsley and serve.

BUTTERNUT LOBSTER BISQUE

PREP TIME: 20 minutes | COOK TIME: 45 minutes | TOTAL TIME: 1 hour 5 minutes
YIELD: 4 to 6 servings

This is definitely a special-occasion soup. It combines three of my favorite things: sweet butternut squash, delicate lobster meat, and creamy bisque. It's a rich bisque; you don't need a large portion. It's a wonderful appetizer before a celebratory meal or a romantic dinner. Save time by purchasing butternut squash that has already been peeled and diced, and lobster meat that has already been cooked.

1 tablespoon extra-virgin olive oil

2 leeks, pale green and white parts only, sliced thin (approximately 2 cups)

1 medium shallot, minced (approximately ½ cup)

3 ribs celery, diced (approximately 1 cup)

4 cups butternut squash, peeled and diced (approximately ½ large)

⅓ cup plus 1 tablespoon cognac

1½ cups seafood stock, preferably homemade (page 17)

Leaves from 1 sprig thyme

1 cup half-and-half, or ½ cup whole milk plus ½ cup heavy cream

½ teaspoon kosher salt, plus a pinch

Ground black pepper

Pinch of cayenne

1 cup cooked lobster meat, chopped

1. Heat the olive oil in a Dutch oven or large heavy-bottom saucepan over low heat. Add the leeks, shallot, and celery with a pinch of salt. Allow the vegetables to sweat for several minutes, stirring periodically, until softened. Add the squash and cook for several more minutes, stirring.

2. Turn the heat to medium and stir less often to allow a brown glaze to build slowly on the bottom of the pan. Use a spatula to scrape up and incorporate the brown bits. After several minutes, add the ⅓ cup cognac to deglaze the pan and loosen the rest of the brown bits. Allow the alcohol to reduce to almost nothing, stirring the vegetables frequently, and then add the stock and thyme.

3. Bring the liquid to a boil, cover the pot, and reduce the heat to low. Allow the soup to simmer for 45 minutes.

4. Carefully transfer the soup to a blender and puree until very smooth. Wipe down the Dutch oven and return the soup to the pot. Stir in the half-and-half, the 1 tablespoon cognac, and the ½ teaspoon salt, black pepper, and cayenne. Add the lobster meat, reserving some for garnish if you prefer. Serve hot.

Note: To reheat the soup, strain out the lobster meat first to avoid overcooking it. Add it once the soup has been heated.

CAULIFLOWER BACON SOUP

PREP TIME: 30 minutes | **COOK TIME:** 1 hour | **TOTAL TIME:** 1 hour 30 minutes
YIELD: 4 to 6 servings

Cauliflower is such a versatile ingredient and it works well as a replacement for cream (and sometimes along with cream to lighten up a dish without removing the fat entirely). It works wonderfully in creamy sauces and soups such as this one. The soup has the smoothness and thickness of a cream or potato soup, but overall it's much lighter. There's still plenty of richness from the bacon. But cauliflower keeps this soup from being over-the-top sinful and a bit more nutritious. And it is very tasty.

5 strips uncooked bacon, diced small

1½ cups chopped yellow onion (approximately 1 large)

¾ cups chopped celery (approximately 2 ribs)

Kosher salt

¼ cup dry white wine

2 cloves garlic, smashed

1 head cauliflower, chopped

3 cups chicken stock, preferably homemade (page 15)

½ cup whole milk (plus more to thin, if desired)

Ground black pepper

1. In a large Dutch oven or heavy-bottom saucepan, render some of the fat from the bacon over low heat for several minutes. Once there's a solid layer of fat in the pan, turn the heat to medium-low and cook the bacon until crisp. Use tongs to remove the bacon and allow it to drain on paper towels. Discard all but approximately 3 tablespoons of the bacon fat (don't worry if there's less than 3 tablespoons; some brands are less fatty than others).

2. Keep a small cup of water nearby. Add the onion and celery to the pan with a pinch of salt and sweat the vegetables for several minutes on medium-low heat. A brown glaze will begin forming on the bottom of the pan. Add 1 tablespoon of the reserved water to deglaze, stirring the brown bits back into the vegetables. Repeat this process for 10 minutes, until the vegetables have caramelized nicely, then deglaze with the wine.

3. Add the garlic and cauliflower, and turn the heat to medium. Cook for approximately 5 minutes, stirring periodically, until the cauliflower has softened. Add the chicken stock and bring the mixture to a boil. Reduce the heat to low and cover. Allow the soup to simmer on low heat for 60 minutes.

recipe continued on page 68

4. Carefully ladle the soup into a blender and puree, in batches if necessary, until silky. Return the soup to the pan and add the milk. Season with salt and pepper to taste.

5. Reheat the reserved bacon briefly in a sauté pan and use it to garnish each bowl of soup.

ROASTED HEIRLOOM TOMATO SOUP WITH SOURDOUGH GRUYÈRE CROUTONS

PREP TIME: 25 minutes | COOK TIME: 1 hour 35 minutes | TOTAL TIME: 2 hours | YIELD: 4 to 6 servings

Homemade tomato soup is so much better than the canned condensed version I grew up with. When tomatoes are out of season, it's fine to make soup using canned tomatoes; they're the superior product. But when tomatoes are at their peak, I love roasting them for an incredibly rich, satisfying soup. If heirlooms aren't available, you can use your favorite local variety.

FOR THE SOUP:

1 small head garlic

¼ cup plus 1 teaspoon plus 1 tablespoon extra-virgin olive oil

1½ teaspoons kosher salt, plus more for seasoning

4½ to 5 pounds heirloom tomatoes of assorted sizes and colors, cored and halved

3 cups chopped yellow onion (approximately 2 large)

2 cups chicken or vegetable stock, preferably homemade (pages 15 and 16)

¼ cup fresh basil, chopped

FOR THE CROUTONS:

3 cups day-old sourdough bread, cut into 1-inch cubes

1½ teaspoons extra-virgin olive oil

1 cup freshly grated Gruyère cheese

1. Preheat the oven to 425°F and line one large or two small baking sheets with aluminum foil.

2. Peel the excess papery layers from the garlic bulb without separating the cloves from the base. Carefully slice off the top of the head so the tip of each individual clove is exposed. Place the garlic on a piece of aluminum foil and drizzle with 1 teaspoon olive oil. Sprinkle with a pinch of salt and wrap the foil tightly around the garlic.

3. Place the tomatoes cut side up on the baking sheet and rub them with a mixture of ¼ cup olive oil and 1½ teaspoons kosher salt. Place the wrapped garlic on the baking sheet. Roast the tomatoes and garlic for 50 minutes.

4. While the tomatoes and garlic are roasting, heat the remaining tablespoon oil in a large saucepan or Dutch oven over medium-low heat. Keep a liquid measuring cup full of water nearby. Add the onions and a pinch of salt to the pan and cook, stirring frequently, until the onion begin to brown. Turn up the heat to medium and continue caramelizing the onion. As a glaze develops on the bottom of the pan, add a few tablespoons of water and scrape up the brown bits, incorporating them into the onion. The heat will cause the water to evaporate. Repeat this process for 25 to 30 minutes, keeping a close eye on the onion to make sure it doesn't

recipe continued on page 71

burn. When the onion has turned a dark brown color and is both bitter and sweet in flavor, remove the pan from the heat and set aside.

5. Remove the tomatoes and garlic from the oven and allow to cool briefly. Carefully remove the foil from the garlic. When the garlic is cool enough to handle, squeeze the roasted garlic cloves out of their skins and into the pan with the caramelized onion. Add the tomatoes, any liquid from the baking sheet, and the chicken stock.

6. Bring the mixture to a boil and then reduce the heat to low and simmer, uncovered, for 30 minutes. Add the basil and simmer for another 5 minutes. Puree with an immersion blender, being careful to retain a bit of texture. For a smoother soup, use a standard blender. For a thicker soup, simmer uncovered for an additional 10 minutes before blending. If you prefer a thinner soup, add more stock until the desired consistency is reached before blending. Season with salt and pepper to taste.

7. To prepare the croutons, preheat the oven to 350°F and line a baking sheet with aluminum foil. Spread the cubed bread evenly and drizzle with the 1½ teaspoons olive oil. Evenly distribute the Gruyère on top. Bake for 5 minutes and use a spatula to flip and stir the croutons. As the cheese melts, it won't distribute evenly over the croutons, so don't worry if it looks messy. Flip and stir the croutons two more times for a total of 15 minutes in the oven. Remove and allow to cool so the cheese firms up.

8. Serve the soup hot and garnished with the croutons.

POACHED SALMON SOUP WITH UDON AND MUSHROOMS

PREP TIME: 20 minutes | COOK TIME: 20 minutes | TOTAL TIME: 40 minutes | YIELD: 4 to 6 servings

Luckily for me, Washington, DC, is surrounded by Asian grocery stores. However, I realize not everyone has easy access to ingredients like fresh udon noodles and miso paste. If you can't find all of these products at your grocery store and don't have access to an Asian market, they're all available (and relatively inexpensive to buy) online. Dry noodles may be substituted, and ramen or soba noodles will also work in this recipe. For a richer soup, use a fatty center cut salmon.

1 (12- or 16-ounce) package fresh or precooked udon noodles (dry may be substituted)

¼ cup white miso paste

4 cups seafood, chicken, or vegetable stock, preferably homemade (pages 15–17)

1 clove garlic, smashed

2 teaspoons oyster sauce

1 teaspoon seasoned rice wine vinegar

2 cups thinly sliced cremini mushrooms (button mushrooms may be substituted)

12 ounces fresh salmon, skinned, deboned, and cut into 1-inch cubes

¼ cup thinly sliced scallions

½ teaspoon toasted sesame oil

1. Prepare the udon noodles according to package instructions and set aside.

2. Dissolve the miso in 2 cups of boiling water, whisking to combine. Pour through a fine mesh strainer, into a large Dutch oven or heavy-bottom saucepan. Discard any remaining lumps. Add the stock, garlic, oyster sauce, and vinegar. Bring the mixture to a simmer over medium heat and cook for 5 minutes. Turn the heat to low. Remove the garlic clove and discard.

3. When the soup is just barely simmering, add the mushrooms and salmon to the pot, and continue to cook for 10 minutes, uncovered. Remove the pot from the heat and stir in the scallions, sesame oil, and cooked udon. Allow the mixture to sit for 3 to 5 minutes before serving.

CHILLED SUMMER CORN SOUP

PREP TIME: 3 hours 15 minutes (mostly inactive) | **COOK TIME:** 1 hour
TOTAL TIME: 4 hour 15 minutes (mostly inactive) | **YIELD:** 8 to 10 servings

I cannot remember where I first learned about using cobs to make corn stock (I certainly didn't invent the idea), but it's a brilliant way to use the entire vegetable. I suggest using fresh, local corn if possible. Certain produce—corn, peaches, and cherries, for example—is not meant to be enjoyed year-round. This is one recipe that I highly recommend preparing only when corn is at its peak freshness.

12 medium ears fresh corn

1 tablespoon extra-virgin olive oil

2 cups diced yellow onion (approximately 1 medium)

2 cloves garlic, minced

½ teaspoon kosher salt

2 cups vegetable stock, preferably homemade (page 16)

Ground black pepper

Crème fraîche and chives for garnish (optional)

1. Remove the kernels from each corncob by slicing and place in a bowl. Set aside.

2. Break the corncobs in half and place in a large Dutch oven or stockpot. Cover with 2 quarts of cold water. Bring to a boil and turn the heat to low. Simmer, uncovered, for 40 minutes.

3. While the corncobs are simmering, heat the oil in a large pot over medium-low heat. Add the onion and cook until translucent, approximately 2 minutes, then add the garlic, salt, and reserved corn. Cook for several minutes, until the corn is soft, stirring frequently, then remove from the heat and cover.

4. Once the corncobs have finished simmering, strain the liquid and add 3 cups to the corn mixture along with the vegetable stock. If the corn stock has reduced to less than 3 cups, add more vegetable stock or plain water to substitute. Simmer the ingredients over medium heat for an additional 15 minutes, covered.

5. Ladle the mixture into a blender and puree in batches. Press the soup through a food mill or fine mesh strainer. Season with salt and pepper to taste. If a thinner consistency is desired, add additional stock (use the corn stock if there's any left over).

6. Place in the refrigerator and chill, approximately 3 hours, or overnight. Adjust the seasoning again, if necessary.

7. If using, garnish with crème fraîche and chives before serving.

CANTALOUPE GAZPACHO

PREP TIME: 8 hours (mostly inactive) | **TOTAL TIME:** 8 hours (mostly inactive) | **YIELD:** 4 to 6 servings

Melons are one of the few fruits I don't have on a regular basis, but I really enjoy using them in chilled soup, especially gazpacho. I love fruit gazpachos in general and have made variations of this recipe using watermelon, cherries, peaches, or whatever berries I have on hand. The key is to let the gazpacho chill in the refrigerator overnight so that the flavors have a chance to blend. It's a wonderfully refreshing soup for a hot summer day.

1 ripe cantaloupe, or 2 pounds peeled and seeded

1 medium cucumber, peeled, seeded, and coarsely chopped (approximately 1½ cups)

¼ cup chopped shallot (approximately 1 small)

¼ cup fresh basil

¼ teaspoon minced garlic

3 tablespoons extra-virgin olive oil

2 tablespoons white wine vinegar

1 tablespoon fresh-squeezed lemon juice (approximately ½ lemon)

¼ teaspoon kosher salt

⅛ teaspoon ground black pepper

1. Cut the cantaloupe in half and scoop out the seeds, discarding them. Slice each half into quarters and use a large spoon to scoop the fruit into a blender, discarding the rind.

2. Add the cucumber, shallot, basil, garlic, oil, vinegar, lemon juice, salt, and pepper to the blender. Puree until smooth.

3. Place the soup in a large container with a tight lid and refrigerate overnight to allow the flavors to blend. Taste, and adjust the seasonings, if desired.

SALADS

PEACH PANZANELLA SALAD

PREP TIME: 40 minutes | **COOK TIME:** 10 minutes | **TOTAL TIME:** 50 minutes | **YIELD:** 5 to 6 servings

Panzanella is a Tuscan salad traditionally made from soaked stale bread and tomatoes. Since peaches are at their peak during tomato season, I like adding them to the mix. Stale bread is used because it holds its shape when soaking up the liquid. It does not need to be toasted because it has already dried out. However, you can also use fresh bread and lightly toast it to achieve a similar effect and add some crunch to the salad. If you toast the bread, aim for something softer and less crunchy than croutons. When chopping the tomatoes and peaches, aim for a size that's similar to the cubed bread.

¼ cup extra-virgin olive oil

1½ tablespoons fresh-squeezed lemon juice

1 teaspoon honey

⅛ teaspoon kosher salt

Pinch of ground black pepper

4 cups stale or toasted fresh crusty artisan bread, cut into 2-inch cubes (see note)

4 heirloom tomatoes, cubed

4 ripe peaches, cubed

1 English cucumber, seeded and sliced into ½-inch pieces

2 to 3 tablespoons ripped or coarsely chopped fresh basil

1. To prepare the vinaigrette, place the oil, lemon juice, honey, salt, and pepper in a blender or jar with a tight-fitting lid. Blend or shake vigorously until combined.

2. In a large bowl, gently toss the toasted bread, tomatoes, peaches, cucumber, and basil.

3. Toss approximately three-fourths of the vinaigrette with the salad ingredients and allow everything to sit for 30 minutes so that the flavors can mingle. If desired, drizzle the remaining vinaigrette over the salad just before serving.

Note: To toast fresh bread, preheat the oven to 350°F. Spread the cubes in a single layer on a sheet pan and toast until lightly crisp and golden on the outside, 5 to 10 minutes, stirring once or twice to toast the bread evenly. Remove from the oven and allow to cool.

SWEET POTATO, APPLE, AND AVOCADO SALAD

PREP TIME: 5 minutes | COOK TIME: 10 minutes | TOTAL TIME: 15 minutes | YIELD: 2 servings

This salad has become a staple in my kitchen. It's adapted from a recipe of Lisa Consiglio Ryan's of Whole Health Designs, one of the first health coaches to teach me about how food can impact my energy level and mood. Whenever I start feeling sluggish, I cut back on things like refined sugars, processed foods, and dairy. I focus on incorporating healthy fats, produce, and whole grains into my diet and without fail, I feel better within a few days. This salad always gives me energy, and is a perfect weekday lunch. It's healthy, flavorful, and filling, and I never grow tired of it.

2 sweet potatoes, peeled and cut into ½-inch cubes

¼ cup sunflower seeds

1 apple, unpeeled and sliced (approximately 1 cup)

½ small red onion, chopped (approximately ½ cup)

¼ cup chopped fresh cilantro

¼ cup fresh-squeezed lime juice (3 to 4 limes)

1 tablespoon extra-virgin olive oil

Kosher salt

Ground black pepper

½ avocado, peeled, pitted, and diced

1. Bring a large saucepan of water to a boil and add the sweet potatoes. Cook until soft but not mushy, approximately 10 minutes. Remove from the pot and rinse under cold water to cool. Drain well.

2. Toast the sunflower seeds in a dry skillet over medium-high heat until golden and fragrant, 3 to 5 minutes.

3. Combine the apple, onion, cilantro, and lime juice in a large bowl. Stir in the sweet potatoes and oil; add salt and pepper to taste.

4. Stir in the avocado and toasted sunflower seeds just before serving.

CITRUS-MARINATED BEET SALAD WITH GOAT CHEESE AND PISTACHIOS

PREP TIME: 12 to 48 hours (mostly inactive) | **COOK TIME:** 45 minutes
TOTAL TIME: 12 to 48 hours 45 minutes (mostly inactive) | **YIELD:** 4 servings

I don't think I tried beets until I was in my thirties. I never had them growing up and I honestly had no idea what to do with them. So I ignored them for years. Eventually I tried them, realized I love them, and began roasting my own (which is quite easy, contrary to popular misconception). I leave the skin on while they roast and then use paper towels or kitchen gloves to remove the skin so my hands don't turn pink. These citrus-marinated beets are similar to pickled beets, but with a milder flavor.

FOR THE BEETS:

2 large beets, skin on and scrubbed

2 teaspoons extra-virgin olive oil

1 cup fresh-squeezed orange juice (approximately 3 oranges)

3 tablespoons fresh-squeezed lemon juice (1 to 2 lemons)

1 teaspoon minced shallot

FOR THE SALAD:

4 to 6 cups baby arugula

1 cup crumbled soft goat cheese

¼ cup shelled and toasted pistachios

1 grapefruit, peeled and cut into segments (orange may be substituted)

¼ cup extra-virgin olive oil

1½ tablespoons fresh-squeezed lemon juice (approximately 1 lemon)

Kosher salt

Ground black pepper

PREPARE THE BEETS:

1. Preheat oven to 375°F.

2. Rub each beet with 1 teaspoon of the olive oil. Wrap each beet in a piece of foil and place on a baking sheet. Roast until fork-tender, 45 to 60 minutes depending on the size of the beets.

3. Allow the beets to cool briefly until they can be safely handled. Peel and discard the skins. Slice the beets into eighths.

4. In a small bowl, whisk the orange juice, lemon juice, and shallot. Add the beets and allow to marinate at least overnight, or for up to 48 hours (the longer they sit, the more citrus flavor the beets will absorb).

PREPARE THE SALAD:

1. Remove the beets from the marinade, discarding the liquid. Pat dry with a paper towel.

2. Divide the arugula evenly among four plates. Top each plate evenly with the beets, goat cheese, pistachios, and grapefruit segments.

3. Place the oil and lemon juice along with a pinch of salt and pepper in a jar with a tight-fitting lid. Shake to emulsify and taste. Adjust seasoning if necessary and drizzle the vinaigrette over the salad. Serve immediately.

MEDITERRANEAN SALAD
WITH ROASTED TOMATO VINAIGRETTE

PREP TIME: 5 minutes | **COOK TIME:** 55 minutes | **TOTAL TIME:** 1 hour | **YIELD:** 4 servings

This salad has a lot of ingredients, but they all work harmoniously to create a flavorful, satisfying meal. It makes a wonderful main course, especially if you add some additional protein, like shredded rotisserie chicken. This roasted tomato vinaigrette is a favorite in our home. It's great on salads but also tastes wonderful over eggs in the morning. I've dipped chicken tenders into this dressing and also served it over steak. It would go perfectly on sandwiches in place of ketchup. It's a bit of a vinaigrette/sauce hybrid.

FOR THE VINAIGRETTE:

1 (14½-ounce) can whole peeled tomatoes

¼ cup extra-virgin olive oil, plus extra for coating

1 tablespoon balsamic vinegar

1 tablespoon red wine vinegar

¼ teaspoon kosher salt

Ground black pepper

FOR THE SALAD:

1 piece pita bread, sliced into wedges

¼ cup dried apricots

4 cups baby arugula

¼ cup pine nuts, toasted

¼ cup cooked white beans, such as cannellini

2 tablespoons pitted black kalamata olives, sliced

1½ tablespoons chopped fresh mint

2 tablespoons crumbled feta cheese

¼ cup cooked farro or barley (optional)

1. Preheat the oven to 350°F and line a baking sheet with aluminum foil. Drain the tomatoes, reserving 2 tablespoons of juice from the can. Slice the tomatoes in half lengthwise and gently squeeze out some of the juice and seeds. Place on the baking sheet and lightly coat the tomatoes with oil. Roast for 45 minutes, stirring the tomatoes halfway through to prevent sticking.

2. In a blender, add the roasted tomatoes, the ¼ cup oil, the vinegars, reserved tomato juice, salt, and a pinch of pepper. Puree until smooth. (The vinaigrette may separate with time, so leave it in the blender and mix again right before serving.)

3. Place the pita bread wedges on a baking sheet and coat with oil. Sprinkle with salt and bake until crisp, approximately 10 minutes.

4. Reconstitute the apricots in boiling water until they soften slightly, 5 to 10 minutes. Drain and slice the apricots into thin strips.

5. Divide a generous portion of baby arugula among four plates. Top with the apricots, pine nuts, beans, olives, mint, feta, and farro, if using.

6. Drizzle the vinaigrette on each salad before serving.

SESAME-CRUSTED TOFU SALAD
WITH SPICY PEANUT DRESSING

PREP TIME: 1 hour | **COOK TIME:** 10 minutes | **TOTAL TIME:** 1 hour 10 minutes | **YIELD:** 3 to 4 servings

Tofu is an excellent way to add heft and protein to salads. When the water is thoroughly drained out of it, tofu absorbs the flavors of marinades wonderfully. It crisps up quite nicely when pan-fried. The texture is reminiscent of paneer cheese, a delicacy I often order at Indian restaurants. Serve this salad for lunch or a light dinner.

FOR THE TOFU:

1 block extra-firm tofu packed in water

2 cloves garlic, smashed

2 tablespoons toasted sesame oil

2 tablespoons soy sauce

2 tablespoons seasoned rice wine vinegar

1 teaspoon crushed red pepper flakes

¼ cup toasted white sesame seeds

1½ tablespoons black sesame seeds

FOR THE DRESSING:

2 tablespoons creamy peanut butter

1 tablespoon soy sauce

1½ teaspoons toasted sesame oil

1 tablespoon seasoned rice vinegar

1½ teaspoons Sriracha hot sauce

½ teaspoon honey or light agave nectar

1 tablespoon water

FOR THE SALAD:

4 cups mixed greens

3 to 4 tablespoons roasted unsalted peanuts

3 to 4 tablespoons thinly sliced scallions

1. To prepare the tofu, remove the tofu from its packaging and discard the water. Line a plate with paper towels and place the tofu on top. Set a small plate on top of the tofu and weight it down with something heavy like a large can or book. Let sit for at least 30 minutes. Drain excess liquid and pat dry. Slice into 1-inch cubes.

2. Add the garlic, oil, soy sauce, vinegar, red pepper flakes, and tofu to a large plastic bag. Seal and chill in the refrigerator for 30 minutes to an hour.

3. To prepare the dressing, while the tofu is marinating, whisk all the ingredients in a medium bowl and set aside.

4. Mix the white and black sesame seeds in a small bowl. Dredge each piece of tofu in the sesame seeds.

5. Heat a large nonstick pan over medium-low heat. You can add a small amount of oil or cooking spray, but the oil in the marinade should help prevent sticking. Add the tofu and allow it to brown a bit before flipping sides, 3 to 5 minutes per side. Periodically swirl the tofu and keep an eye on the heat to make sure the sesame seeds don't burn.

6. Serve the tofu over mixed greens. Top each salad with peanuts and scallions.

7. Drizzle the spicy peanut dressing over the salad and serve.

ARUGULA AND WHITE BEAN SALAD
WITH PROSCIUTTO AND PARMESAN

PREP TIME: 10 minutes | **COOK TIME:** 15 minutes | **TOTAL TIME:** 25 minutes | **YIELD:** 4 servings

White beans, such as cannellini, navy, and Great Northern, are a wonderful addition to salads, soups, and stews. They have a smooth, creamy texture and a pleasant flavor that's neutral enough to work in a variety of dishes. I love them in this textured salad, which is one of my favorites. As I mentioned at the beginning of the chapter, balance is key in a good salad. Here you have bitterness from the arugula, sourness from the bread and vinaigrette, sweetness from the basil, and saltiness from the prosciutto and cheese. The key to making this basil pepper vinaigrette is blanching the basil. Basil will turn brown very quickly once it's cut, and blanching preserves that beautiful bright green color in the vinaigrette that will elevate even the most basic salad.

FOR THE VINAIGRETTE:
¾ cup packed fresh basil

½ cup extra-virgin olive oil

1 tablespoon balsamic vinegar

1 tablespoon red wine vinegar

1 teaspoon fresh-squeezed
lemon juice

1 teaspoon minced garlic

¼ teaspoon kosher salt

¾ teaspoon ground black
pepper

FOR THE SALAD:
2 cups day-old sourdough
bread, cut into 1-inch cubes

4 cups baby arugula

1 cup cooked white beans,
such as cannellini

12 slices prosciutto, rolled
individually

½ cup shaved Parmigiano-
Reggiano cheese, plus more as
needed

1. To make the vinaigrette, bring a medium pot of water to a boil. Fill a medium bowl with ice water.

2. Add the basil to the boiling water, pushing it below the surface with a slotted spoon so that it blanches evenly. After 15 seconds, use the spoon to scoop out the wilted basil and add it to the ice water to halt the cooking process. Once cold, use paper towels to squeeze out as much water as possible.

3. Place the basil, olive oil, vinegars, lemon juice, garlic, salt, and pepper in a blender and puree on high speed until smooth. The vinaigrette may separate with time, so leave it in the blender and mix again right before serving.

4. To make the salad, preheat the oven to 350°F. Spread the bread in a single layer on a sheet pan and toast until crisp, approximately 10 minutes.

5. Divide the arugula among four plates. Top each plate with ½ cup of the croutons, ¼ cup of the beans, 3 slices of the prosciutto, and Parmigiano-Reggiano to taste.

6. Drizzle the vinaigrette over each salad.

GRILLED ZUCCHINI SALAD WITH FETA AND SWEET CROUTONS

PREP TIME: 5 minutes | **COOK TIME:** 20 minutes | **TOTAL TIME:** 25 minutes | **YIELD:** 4 servings

This is another salad where flavor balance is key. I use baby arugula (my favorite bitter green), Hawaiian sweet rolls, lemon juice, and good-quality feta cheese. I always prefer using the feta blocks that come packed in water as opposed to the crumbled variety. The flavor is more briny, milky, and fresh. It costs a bit more, but it's worth it when you have a dish that relies on just a few basic ingredients. If you've never tried Hawaiian sweet rolls, take note that they're not sugary sweet. They have a light, honey-flavored sweetness. Brioche will also work in this salad, but the sweetness won't be quite as pronounced.

4 Hawaiian sweet rolls, cut into 1-inch cubes (2 cups brioche cubes may be substituted)

¼ cup plus 1 tablespoon extra-virgin olive oil

⅛ teaspoon kosher salt, plus more for seasoning

2 medium zucchini, sliced into quarters lengthwise

1 tablespoon vegetable oil or melted clarified butter for grilling

2 tablespoons fresh-squeezed lemon juice (approximately 1 lemon)

Ground black pepper

4 cups baby arugula

½ cup crumbled feta cheese

1. Preheat the oven to 350°F. Line a baking sheet with aluminum foil.

2. Place the sweet rolls on the baking sheet in a single layer. Drizzle with the 1 tablespoon olive oil and sprinkle with salt. Toast in the oven, checking every 5 minutes and flipping when the bottoms turn golden so that they crisp evenly. This should take approximately 15 minutes total. Set aside.

3. Preheat a grill until very hot (see note). Brush a light coating of vegetable oil or clarified butter on the zucchini. Place the zucchini slices on the grill and cook for 2 minutes, uncovered, then flip and cook the other sides for an additional 2 minutes.

4. Place the ¼ cup olive oil, lemon juice, salt, and a pinch of pepper in a jar with a tight-fitting lid. Shake vigorously to emulsify the ingredients.

5. Divide the baby arugula onto four salad plates. Top each salad with 2 slices of the zucchini, 2 tablespoons of the feta, and the croutons.

6. Drizzle lightly with the vinaigrette.

Note: A hot grill pan can be used if an outdoor grill is not available.

PEAR, ROQUEFORT, DATE, AND WALNUT SALAD

PREP TIME: 10 minutes | COOK TIME: 5 minutes | TOTAL TIME: 15 minutes | YIELD: 4 servings

The idea for this salad came from a classic appetizer: bacon- or prosciutto-wrapped Medjool dates stuffed with cheese. Pears, blue cheese, and walnuts are very complementary. Honestly, this salad is so flavorful you can skip the vinaigrette if you want to keep things simple. If Bosc pears are unavailable, Bartlett pears are a fine substitute.

¼ cup extra-virgin olive oil

1½ tablespoons white wine vinegar

1 teaspoon Dijon mustard

1 teaspoon honey

⅛ teaspoon kosher salt

⅛ teaspoon ground black pepper

2 slices thick-cut bacon

4 to 6 cups red leaf lettuce, torn into small pieces (or salad greens of your choice)

6 to 8 Medjool dates, pitted and sliced thin

¼ cup walnuts, toasted and coarsely chopped

2 Bosc pears, unpeeled and sliced

½ cup crumbled Roquefort cheese

1. In a blender or jar with a tight-fitting lid, combine the oil, vinegar, mustard, honey, salt, and pepper. Puree or shake vigorously to combine. Set aside.

2. Slice the bacon into ¼-inch pieces. Place in a medium sauté pan and cook over low heat to render the fat, stirring periodically, then turn up the heat and cook for several more minutes, until golden and crisp. Using a slotted spoon, remove to a plate lined with paper towels and briefly allow the fat to drain.

3. In a large serving bowl, combine the lettuce, dates, walnuts, and pears. Drizzle with a small amount of the dressing and gently toss to combine. Taste and add more dressing, if desired. Divide among four plates and top evenly with the Roquefort and bacon.

GRILLED SKIRT STEAK SALAD
WITH TAHINI DRESSING

PREP TIME: 15 minutes | **COOK TIME:** 6 minutes | **TOTAL TIME:** 21 minutes | **YIELD:** 4 servings

Tahini is an extremely versatile condiment. In addition to having a unique and wonderful flavor, it easily can be used in both savory and sweet recipes. I use it in dips, dressings, sauces, cookies, and buttercream frosting. I've even used it to make ice cream! Here I've included it in one of my favorite dressings that I also often use as an all-purpose sauce. It pairs especially well with both meats and vegetables, so I often add it to wraps. While I use skirt steak in this recipe, flank and flat iron steak also work well. This satisfying steak salad is perfect for lunch or dinner.

FOR THE DRESSING:

¼ cup extra-virgin olive oil

3 tablespoons well-stirred tahini

3 tablespoons fresh-squeezed lemon juice (approximately 1 lemon)

1 tablespoon tamari

1 small or ½ medium clove garlic

½ teaspoon crushed red pepper flakes

FOR THE SALAD:

¾ pound skirt steak

Vegetable oil or melted clarified butter for grilling

Kosher salt

Ground black pepper

4 to 6 cups baby arugula

1. To prepare the dressing, puree the olive oil, tahini, lemon juice, tamari, garlic, and red pepper flakes in a blender. Add additional salt to taste, if desired.

2. To prepare the salad, reheat a grill on high heat. Rub vegetable oil on both sides of the skirt steak and season with salt and pepper.

3. Grill the steak on high heat for 3 minutes per side with the lid closed. Allow the steak to rest for at least 5 minutes and then slice against the grain into strips.

4. Right before serving, layer the steak over the baby arugula and top with the dressing.

QUINOA, BLUEBERRY, AND ALMOND SALAD WITH HONEY LEMON MINT VINAIGRETTE

PREP TIME: 20 minutes | **COOK TIME:** 15 minutes | **TOTAL TIME:** 35 minutes | **YIELD:** 6 to 8 servings

I could eat this salad for lunch every day during our hot and humid summer months in Washington, DC. While I love the combination of blueberries, almonds, mint, and quinoa, you could certainly try replacing these ingredients with your favorite berries, nuts, and whole grains. Don't skip triple soaking the quinoa. It often has an unpleasant flavor that will stick around if you don't properly rinse it.

FOR THE VINAIGRETTE:

3 tablespoons honey

2 tablespoons packed fresh mint

⅓ cup fresh-squeezed lemon juice (approximately 3 lemons)

2 tablespoons water

¼ cup extra-virgin olive oil

⅛ teaspoon kosher salt

Ground black pepper

FOR THE SALAD:

1½ cups uncooked quinoa

¼ teaspoon kosher salt, plus a pinch

½ cup thinly sliced scallions

1½ cups fresh blueberries

½ cup toasted almonds, coarsely chopped

1 tablespoon coarsely chopped packed fresh mint

Ground black pepper

1. To prepare the vinaigrette, puree the honey, mint, lemon juice, water, oil, salt, and pepper in a blender. Set aside.

2. Place the quinoa in a fine mesh strainer and place the strainer in a large bowl. Fill the bowl with cold water and allow the quinoa to soak for 5 minutes. Remove the strainer with the quinoa and drain the water from the bowl. Repeat this process two more times for a total of three washes over 15 minutes. This will help remove a potentially unpleasant aftertaste from the quinoa.

3. Combine the quinoa with 3 cups of water and a pinch of salt in a medium saucepan, and bring to a boil. Reduce to low heat and cover. Simmer for 15 minutes.

4. Move the quinoa to a large bowl and allow it to cool for 5 minutes. Add the scallions, blueberries, almonds, mint, salt, and pepper. Gently toss to combine.

5. Briefly whisk the vinaigrette ingredients in a small bowl and then pour over the quinoa mixture, tossing to combine with the other ingredients.

ARUGULA AND NECTARINE SALAD

PREP TIME: 10 minutes | **TOTAL TIME:** 10 minutes | **YIELD:** 4 servings

Every summer I look forward to fresh nectarines and peaches. They're so good by themselves, but I also love using them in desserts and adding them to salads. You could definitely use peaches in this salad, but I really enjoy the way nectarines taste with Gorgonzola. I've listed it as an optional ingredient, because if you want a lighter version of this salad, it's still excellent without the cheese. Salty blue Gorgonzola with sweet, juicy nectarines is an epic combination. Toasted slivered almonds add just the right amount of crunch.

¼ cup extra-virgin olive oil

1½ tablespoons white wine vinegar

1 teaspoon Dijon mustard

1 teaspoon honey

⅛ teaspoon kosher salt

⅛ teaspoon ground black pepper

6 cups baby arugula

2 ripe nectarines (peeled or unpeeled), pitted and sliced

½ cup toasted slivered almonds

¼ cup crumbled Gorgonzola cheese (optional)

1. In a blender or jar with a tight-fitting lid, combine the oil, vinegar, mustard, honey, salt, and pepper. Puree or shake vigorously to combine. Set aside.

2. Divide the arugula evenly among four plates and top with the nectarines, almonds, and Gorgonzola, if using. Drizzle with the vinaigrette to taste and serve.

APPETIZERS AND SIDES

Small plates have become a popular trend in recent years at both restaurants and home gatherings. I appreciate this because I'm an indecisive diner and often struggle with what to order. Even when I'm dining at restaurants that don't specialize in small plates, sometimes I opt for a few appetizers instead of an entrée. I like to try a little bit of everything. These recipes are perfect for entertaining guests buffet style or serving alongside both large and intimate dinners.

APPETIZERS

LOADED HUMMUS

PREP TIME: 10 minutes | **COOK TIME:** 5 minutes | **TOTAL TIME:** 15 minutes | **YIELD:** approximately 2½ cups

Homemade hummus is delicious and easy to prepare, even for the novice chef. I like keeping it around for a healthy snack, and it's a fast, easy appetizer to whip up for guests. This is a fun Mediterranean twist on my standard recipe. It yields the right amount of topping for the hummus, but might be overkill for serving all at once depending on the size and width of the serving bowl, so you might want to use two smaller bowls or a long, shallow dish. Hummus is typically prepared using garbanzo beans (also known as chickpeas), but I prefer to use white beans because of their smoother consistency. I typically use cannellinis, but navy or Great Northern beans work just as well.

1 (14½-ounce) can white beans, drained

½ cup well-stirred tahini

1 small or ½ large clove garlic, minced

¼ cup extra-virgin olive oil

¼ cup water

1 tablespoon fresh-squeezed lemon juice (approximately ½ lemon)

1 teaspoon kosher salt

Ground black pepper

Pita bread for serving (optional)

¼ cup crumbled good-quality feta

2 tablespoons thinly sliced kalamata olives

4 sun-dried tomatoes packed in olive oil, drained and julienned

¼ cup toasted pine nuts

1 tablespoon chopped fresh parsley

1. Place the beans, tahini, garlic, oil, water, lemon juice, salt, and pepper in a food processor. Pulse the machine several times and then puree the ingredients until very smooth. Taste and adjust the seasonings, if desired.

2. If serving with pita, preheat the oven to 350°F. Cut several rounds of the bread into wedges and place on a baking sheet. Toast until crisp, 5 to 7 minutes.

3. Place the hummus in a large serving bowl and top with the feta, olives, sun-dried tomatoes, pine nuts, and parsley. Serve with pita bread, if using.

BOURSIN DEVILED EGGS

PREP TIME: 10 minutes | **COOK TIME:** 15 minutes | **TOTAL TIME:** 25 minutes | **YIELDS:** 24 deviled eggs

Boursin is a spreadable cheese from France that has been around for years and is widely available in stores. It has a delicate texture similar to whipped cream cheese, but has a more neutral flavor that sets the stage for a mixture of herbs and spices. Because both the cheese and the egg yolks are rich, I like cutting the heaviness with some Greek yogurt, which keeps the texture smooth and creamy while lightening up the overall consistency.

12 large eggs

½ cup plain Greek yogurt

1 cup Boursin Garlic & Fine Herbs cheese

1½ teaspoons fresh-squeezed lemon juice

½ teaspoon kosher salt

¼ teaspoon ground black pepper

3 tablespoons whole wheat bread crumbs or panko bread crumbs

1. Bring a large pot of water to a rolling boil. Gently add the eggs and cook for exactly 12 minutes, then place the eggs directly into an ice bath until cool. Peel the eggs and slice in half using a sharp knife. Scoop the yolks into a large bowl, taking care to leave the whites intact.

2. Arrange an oven rack in the highest position and preheat the broiler to low.

3. Mash the yolks, yogurt, cheese, lemon juice, salt, and pepper. Scoop the mixture into the egg whites and set on a baking sheet.

4. Sprinkle the bread crumbs evenly over the eggs and place them under the broiler. Toast, watching carefully to make sure the bread crumbs don't burn, 2 to 3 minutes.

BAKED BRIE WITH BLACKBERRY COMPOTE AND SPICY CANDIED PECANS

PREP TIME: 10 minutes | **COOK TIME:** 40 minutes | **TOTAL TIME:** 50 minutes | **YIELD:** approximately 10 servings

When I was younger, my mother used to make a two-ingredient appetizer for guests: Gouda cheese baked in flaky, golden crescent roll dough. Baked Brie always reminds me of that dish, but with a sweet and savory twist. If you want to keep things simple, you can bake the Brie exactly as I've described in the final steps and serve it with plain berries and toasted, salted nuts.

1 cup pecan pieces or halves

½ tablespoon unsalted butter

1½ tablespoons light brown sugar

2 teaspoons pure maple syrup

¼ teaspoon ground cinnamon

¾ teaspoons kosher salt

¼ teaspoon cayenne

2 cups blackberries, plus extra for garnish

1 tablespoon fresh-squeezed lemon juice (approximately ½ lemon)

1 teaspoon pure vanilla extract

1 tablespoon honey

1 (15-ounce) or 2 (8-ounce) wheels Brie, room temperature

Crackers for serving

1. To prepare the candied pecans, preheat the oven to 350°F. Line a baking sheet with aluminum foil and lightly grease with cooking spray. Spread the pecans in a single layer and toast in the oven until golden and fragrant, approximately 10 minutes. Stir every 3 or 4 minutes.

2. While the pecans are toasting, prepare the coating mixture. Microwave the butter in a large microwave-safe bowl until melted. Stir in the brown sugar, maple syrup, cinnamon, salt, and cayenne.

3. Pour the hot nuts into the coating mixture. (Be careful, as it might sputter and hiss.) Stir until the nuts are evenly coated, pour back onto the baking sheet, and spread them in an even layer.

4. Bake for another 10 minutes, stirring every 3 or 4 minutes. Remove from the oven and allow to cool. Once cool, break the nuts apart or chop them coarsely.

5. In a medium saucepan, heat the blackberries, lemon juice, vanilla, and honey over medium-low heat, stirring periodically. As liquid begins to release from the berries, turn the heat up to medium.

6. Cook, stirring periodically, until the liquid is syrupy and reduced, 10 to 15 minutes.

7. Preheat the oven to 350°F and line a baking sheet with aluminum foil.

8. Carefully slice away the top of the Brie rind and discard (do not cut down the sides of the rind; it contains the melted cheese). Bake for 15 minutes or until melted through.

9. Top with the berry compote and candied pecans and serve with crackers.

ROASTED CHERRY, FETA, AND MINT CROSTINI

PREP TIME: 20 minutes | **COOK TIME:** 25 minutes | **TOTAL TIME:** 45 minutes | **YIELD:** 20-plus crostini

Crostini is always a great appetizer to prepare for large groups. It can be thrown together without too much effort. This colorful version packs big flavor into each bite. Sweet roasted cherries contrast nicely with the fresh mint and salty feta cheese. While you can use crumbled feta here, I like using thinly sliced feta fresh out of the brine. It's extra salty and, in my opinion, makes for a nicer presentation. Pitting cherries can be a slow, messy ordeal; use a cherry pitter and food gloves for a faster, tidier process.

1 pound sweet cherries, pitted

1 French baguette, sliced thin diagonally (about ½-inch slices)

¼-pound block good-quality feta packed in water

1 bunch fresh mint leaves, whole or sliced thin (approximately 2 cups)

1. Preheat the oven to 400°F and line a baking sheet with aluminum foil. Place the cherries on the baking sheet and roast, shaking the baking sheet every 4 minutes, until the cherries are juicy and soft, approximately 16 minutes. Allow to cool.

2. Lower the oven temperature to 350°F and toast the baguette slices until crisp and golden, 7 to 10 minutes.

3. Drain the feta on paper towels. Slice into thin strips and layer on the bread. Top with the roasted cherries and mint.

SHRIMP, MANGO, AND AVOCADO SUMMER ROLLS

PREP TIME: 30 minutes | **TOTAL TIME:** 30 minutes | **YIELD:** 10 rolls

Homemade summer rolls sound and look fancy, but they're not difficult to make. Rice paper wrappers can be found in the international aisle of most grocery stores. The wrappers can be brittle before dipping in water, so even though the recipe calls for ten, I recommend having some extra on hand. To save time when preparing this recipe, I purchase shrimp that have already been cooked, peeled, and deveined. There will likely be some leftover avocado and mango slices. Better to have a bit extra than not enough!

Vegetable oil, or any neutral-flavored, high-heat oil, for coating

FOR THE SUMMER ROLLS:

20 medium shrimp, peeled, deveined, and cooked, sliced in half lengthwise

2 avocados, peeled, pitted, and sliced into thin strips

2 mangoes, peeled, pitted, and sliced into thin strips

2 scallions, sliced diagonally

½ cup packed cilantro leaves

A handful of mung bean sprouts

1 lime, halved

10 rice paper wrappers

FOR THE DIPPING SAUCE:

3 tablespoons creamy peanut butter

3 tablespoons seasoned rice wine vinegar

1½ tablespoons tamari

1 tablespoon honey

1 tablespoon water

1. Create a rolling station for the summer rolls with six bowls, one each for the shrimp, avocados, mangoes, scallions, cilantro, and bean sprouts. Set out a large cutting board. Place a second large cutting board or plate nearby; brush it lightly with a small amount of oil.

2. Gently toss the avocados with lime juice to keep them from turning brown.

3. Wet a rice paper wrapper in cold water for 3 to 5 seconds. This can be done either directly in the sink or by dipping it into a pie dish filled with cold water. Place the wrapper on the ungreased cutting board.

4. Spread approximately 1 tablespoon of cilantro leaves lengthwise in the center of the wrapper, about the length you want the finished roll to be. Top with 4 shrimp halves, followed by 2 to 3 slices of avocado, 2 to 3 slices of mango, a light sprinkle of scallions, and a few bean sprouts. Take care not to overfill the rolls. Remember the quantity of filling should depend on the size of the avocado and mango slices, which will be uneven due to their natural rounded shape.

5. Carefully fold the bottom of the wrapper over the filling and then fold the right and left sides in, trying to keep

recipe continued on page 112

the filling tightly in place. Roll the summer roll tightly upward until it's sealed. Place on the oiled cutting board (the oil will prevent the rolls from sticking).

6. Repeat this process with the remaining ingredients (see note).

7. In a medium bowl, whisk the peanut butter, vinegar, tamari, honey, and water until smooth. Serve with the summer rolls.

Note: Summer rolls can be stored in an airtight container in the refrigerator for up to 3 days.

APPLE, CHEDDAR, AND CARAMELIZED ONION GALETTE

PREP TIME: 2 hours 30 minutes (mostly inactive) | **COOK TIME:** 1 hour
TOTAL TIME: 3 hour 30 minutes (mostly inactive) | **YIELD:** 6 to 8 servings

Some of my favorite recipes combine both sweet and savory elements, and this lovely autumn tart is a perfect example of why. Apples, cheddar, and caramelized onions are all very complementary, and whole wheat flour adds a nice earthiness. Using whole wheat flour creates a slightly grainer crust than traditional dough; you can adjust the ratio of whole wheat to all-purpose flour for a smoother consistency.

FOR THE DOUGH:

2½ ounces (½ cup) all-purpose flour

2½ ounces (½ cup) whole wheat flour

3 ounces (6 tablespoons) unsalted butter, cold and cut into small pieces

½ teaspoon kosher salt

3 tablespoons ice water

FOR THE FILLING:

1½ teaspoons extra-virgin olive oil

1 large yellow onion sliced thin (approximately 3 cups)

¾ cup shredded mild cheddar cheese

1 tart apple, such as Granny Smith

Kosher salt

Ground black pepper

1. Add the flours, butter, and salt to a food processor. Pulse on and off until the mixture is crumbly. Slowly add the water with the machine running just until the dough forms a ball.

2. Place the dough in plastic wrap and flatten into a disk. Chill for at least 2 hours or overnight.

3. Heat the oil on low in a large skillet. Keep a liquid measuring cup full of water nearby. Add the onion with a pinch of salt. Sweat the onion, stirring, until it begins to caramelize. Turn the heat up to medium-low. Once a brown glaze has formed on the bottom of the skillet, pour approximately 2 to 3 tablespoons of water into the pan to deglaze and use a spatula to scrape up the brown bits and stir them into the onion.

4. Repeat this glazing and deglazing process until the onion has been thoroughly caramelized and taste both sweet and bitter, 25 to 35 minutes. Use more or less water as needed. Set the caramelized onion aside.

5. Preheat the oven to 375°F. Line a baking sheet with parchment paper.

6. Roll the dough onto a lightly floured surface until thin, approximately ¼ inch. Use a pizza cutter to make a circle

recipe continued on page 115

with the dough that's approximately 12 inches in diameter. Carefully transfer the rolled dough to the baking sheet.

7. Distribute the cheese evenly onto the dough, leaving approximately 2 inches around the border. Top with the caramelized onion.

8. Core the apple and slice it in half. Slice each half into very thin pieces. Fan the apple slices decoratively on top of the onion. Top with a light sprinkle of salt and pepper. Fold the excess dough on top of the ingredients until you have a tightly formed tart.

9. Bake the galette until the dough is golden and firm, 18 to 22 minutes. Serve immediately.

GRILLED OYSTERS WITH CHIPOTLE-TARRAGON BUTTER AND GREMOLATA

PREP TIME: 30 minutes | **COOK TIME:** 4 minutes | **TOTAL TIME:** 34 minutes | **YIELD:** 12 oysters

Raw oysters are a wonderful delicacy, but there's something about the smokiness of a hot grilled oyster that I love even more. This recipe has a fancy-sounding name, but the most difficult part is shucking the oysters. Gremolata refers to a garnish made from chopped parsley, garlic, and grated lemon zest. Compound butters are simply regular butter combined with other ingredients such as herbs and spices. Compound butters and gremolata are fast and easy to prepare and the oysters take only 3 to 4 minutes on the grill. Remember that it's much better to undercook than to overcook the oysters, as they can become chewy quickly. The sizzling butter will fry the oysters and the gremolata adds a zesty freshness. Be sure to save any leftover gremolata! It's an excellent condiment to serve over meat, seafood, pasta, or vegetables.

4 ounces (8 tablespoons) unsalted butter, room temperature

1 tablespoon chipotle chilies in adobo sauce, patted dry and minced

1 tablespoon finely chopped fresh tarragon

¼ teaspoon kosher salt

½ cup loosely packed fresh parsley, finely chopped

2½ teaspoons grated lemon zest

1 medium clove garlic, minced or grated

12 raw oysters, scrubbed clean

1. In a medium bowl, combine the butter, chilies, tarragon, and salt, using a spatula to press the ingredients together until evenly blended. Let the butter firm up in the refrigerator while preparing the other ingredients.

2. Combine the parsley, lemon zest, and garlic in a small bowl to make the gremolata.

3. Preheat the grill to medium-high. While the grill is heating, shuck the oysters. If you get any grit in the shell, rinse it briefly. Discard the flat side of the shell, and line up the oysters on a baking sheet.

4. Top each oyster with approximately ½ to 1 tablespoon of the chipotle-tarragon butter. Adjust the quantity based on the size of the oyster and shell.

5. Using tongs, carefully place each oyster directly on the grill shell side down and close the lid. Cook for 3 to 4 minutes, no longer.

6. Use tongs to place the oysters back on the baking sheet. Hot butter might drip depending on the shape of the shells, so be careful.

7. Sprinkle a small amount of gremolata over each oyster and serve immediately.

MUSHROOM DUMPLINGS

PREP TIME: 30 minutes | COOK TIME: 10 minutes | TOTAL TIME: 40 minutes
YIELD: Approximately 20 dumplings

Dumplings, also known as pot stickers or gyoza, just might be one of my favorite snacks. They also make a great appetizer. I am lucky to live near some Asian markets and I often stock up on packaged frozen dumplings. But when there is time, homemade is best. I have used button mushrooms in this recipe, but most varieties will work. You can also experiment with a blend. Shiitake and oyster mushrooms are a great filling for dumplings. Sambal, though not essential, is a very flavorful chili pepper condiment that can be found in the international aisle of most grocery stores. It adds a nice heat and complexity without overpowering the other ingredients.

1½ teaspoons extra-virgin olive oil

⅛ teaspoon kosher salt

2 cups chopped button mushrooms

2 cloves garlic, minced

2 tablespoons thinly sliced scallions

½ teaspoon soy sauce, plus more for dipping

1 teaspoon toasted sesame oil

½ teaspoon sambal oelek (optional)

Small round dumpling wrappers

Vegetable oil for frying

1. Heat the olive oil and salt in a skillet over medium-low heat. Add the mushrooms and allow them to sweat for several minutes, stirring periodically. Once most of the water is evaporated, turn the heat up to medium and add the garlic. Cook for another 1 to 2 minutes, or until the garlic is fragrant. Remove from the heat and allow the mixture to cool.

2. In a medium bowl, combine the mushrooms, scallions, soy sauce, sesame oil, and sambal, if using.

3. Fill a small bowl with water. Wet the edges of a dumpling wrapper. Place a teaspoon of mushroom filling in the wrapper, fold in half, and press firmly to close. The wrapper can be either simply pinched together or decoratively pleated by hand. Place on a baking sheet and repeat with the remaining ingredients.

4. Heat approximately 1 tablespoon of vegetable oil in a skillet on medium heat. Taking care not to overcrowd the pan, add several dumplings flat side down. Cook for 30 to 60 seconds, until the bottoms are golden, gently swirling the pan to prevent sticking. Add ¼ cup of water, cover the pan, and turn the heat down to low. (Be careful, as the oil might splatter; I recommend wearing an oven mitt when adding the water.) Cook for another 1 to 2 minutes, until the wrapper is steamed and most of the water has evaporated from the pan. Set the cooked dumplings aside and repeat until all the dumplings are cooked.

5. Serve with soy sauce.

SPINACH, ARTICHOKE, AND CARAMELIZED LEEK TART

PREP TIME: 15 minutes | **COOK TIME:** 45 minutes | **TOTAL TIME:** 1 hour | **YIELD:** 8 to 10 servings

This tart is a great option for serving at parties because you can prepare the components up to twenty-four hours in advance. An hour before the event, you can roll out the dough, layer the ingredients, and bake the tart so it's ready as people arrive. Make sure to drain the artichokes and spinach before placing them on the puff pastry dough to avoid excess liquid.

1 tablespoon unsalted butter

2 cups chopped leeks, white and pale green parts only (approximately 1½ to 2 leeks)

Kosher salt

4 to 5 cups fresh spinach

Ground black pepper

1 (14-ounce) can artichoke quarters, drained and patted dry

1 sheet puff pastry, chilled

¼ cup freshly grated Parmigiano-Reggiano cheese

1. Preheat the oven to 400°F and line a baking sheet with parchment paper. Set aside.

2. Heat the butter in a large skillet over low heat. Keep a small cup of water nearby. Add the leeks with a pinch of salt. Sweat for 2 to 3 minutes, stirring, then turn the heat to medium and begin caramelizing the leeks. As a brown glaze forms on the bottom of the pan, add 1 to 2 tablespoons of water at a time and stir to incorporate the glaze back into the leeks. Once they are nicely caramelized, 10 to 15 minutes, remove from the heat.

3. Place the spinach in a Dutch oven or large skillet with a splash of water or olive oil. Turn the heat to medium-low, cover, and allow the spinach to wilt, stirring periodically, 2 to 4 minutes. Season with a pinch of salt and pepper and drain on a plate lined with paper towels.

4. Roll out the chilled puff pastry until it is approximately 11 x 15 inches. Place the dough on the baking sheet. Distribute the leeks, spinach, and artichokes evenly, leaving a small border at the edge of the dough. Top with the cheese.

5. Bake the tart for 25 to 30 minutes, or until the edges are golden and firm. Periodically check on the tart while it's cooking. If part of the dough around the edge inflates with an air bubble, gently prick with a fork to deflate.

6. Slice and serve.

SIDES

STEAMED ASPARAGUS
WITH CRÈME FRAÎCHE DRESSING

PREP TIME: 5 minutes | **COOK TIME:** 5 minutes | **TOTAL TIME:** 10 minutes | **YIELD:** 6 to 8 servings

I prefer vegetables roasted, but asparagus is an exception. Asparagus makes an excellent side dish because it's wonderful when steamed and simply tossed with some olive oil, salt, and pepper. For smaller quantities, I don't even bother with a steamer basket; I wrap the asparagus in a damp paper towel and microwave it for approximately 3 minutes on a small plate (the time varies based on the quantity). I learned this trick from Alton Brown and it works beautifully. But for larger quantities I still use a vegetable steamer, and that's what this recipe calls for, though you can certainly use the microwave when scaling down the ingredients. This dressing is reminiscent of a lemony hollandaise but with much less work involved. To make your own crème fraîche, see page 7.

¼ cup plus 2 tablespoons extra-virgin olive oil

2 tablespoons fresh-squeezed lemon juice (approximately 1 lemon)

2½ tablespoons crème fraîche

1 teaspoon chopped fresh dill

½ teaspoon kosher salt

1½ to 2 pounds asparagus, tough ends removed

1. In a medium bowl, whisk the oil, lemon juice, crème fraîche, dill, and salt until smooth. Set aside.

2. Place the asparagus in a steamer basket over simmering water and steam until bright green and tender but not mushy, 2 to 4 minutes (the time will vary depending on the thickness of the asparagus).

3. Arrange the asparagus on a plate and drizzle the dressing on top. Serve hot.

BROCCOLI CHEDDAR BAKED POTATOES

PREP TIME: 10 minutes | **COOK TIME:** 1 hour 15 minutes | **TOTAL TIME:** 1 hour 25 minutes
YIELD: 4 servings

I did not include a recipe for broccoli cheddar soup in the book because there are already a ton of recipes for it, but it's one of my favorites. Broccoli and cheddar combined are so complementary. They add color, texture, and a nice balance of flavors to this baked potato side dish.

4 large russet potatoes

2 cups chopped broccoli florets

½ cup sour cream

1 cup grated sharp cheddar cheese, plus more for topping

3 tablespoons finely chopped fresh chives

½ teaspoon kosher salt

1. Preheat the oven to 400° F. Line a baking sheet with aluminum foil.

2. Pierce the potatoes several times with a fork, place them on the baking sheet, and cook for 1 hour, or until cooked through. Allow to cool briefly.

3. Place the broccoli in a steamer basket over simmering water and steam until tender but not mushy, 3 to 4 minutes.

4. Slice off the top one-third of each potato, setting aside for a different use or discarding. Use a spoon to carefully scoop the potato filling from the bottom halves into a large bowl while leaving the skins intact.

5. Use a potato masher to break down the potatoes. Stir in the sour cream, broccoli, cheese, chives, and salt.

6. Scoop the filling back into each potato. Grate some additional cheddar cheese on top of each potato.

7. Bake for 10 minutes or until heated through. Serve hot.

MAPLE BACON BRUSSELS SPROUTS

PREP TIME: 5 minutes | **COOK TIME:** 20 minutes | **TOTAL TIME:** 25 minutes | **YIELD:** 2 to 3 servings

Brussels sprouts are one of those vegetables that everyone seems to either love or hate. I stand firm in my love of them as long as they are cooked properly. Brussels sprouts are not meant to be boiled in water. They should be caramelized with high heat, either in a sauté pan or roasted in the oven. I often prepare them simply with olive oil, garlic, and balsamic vinegar. But when I want a real treat, I add bacon and maple syrup for a tasty sweet and salty side dish.

1 pound Brussels sprouts

5 slices thick-cut bacon, diced

2 tablespoons balsamic vinegar

2 tablespoons pure maple syrup

Kosher salt

Ground black pepper

1. Cut off the root ends of the Brussels sprouts and remove any loose outer leaves. Slice in half.

2. In a large skillet, render the fat from the bacon over low to medium-low heat. Once the fat has mostly liquefied, turn up the heat to medium-high and cook the bacon until caramelized and crunchy. Set aside to drain on a plate lined with paper towels. Remove all but 2 tablespoons of the bacon fat from the pan.

3. Add the Brussels sprouts to the skillet and caramelize them on one side. Deglaze the pan with the vinegar, using a spatula to scrape up any brown bits and incorporate them with the Brussels sprouts. Continue to sauté the Brussels sprouts on high heat for a few minutes, swirling the pan, until they are tender. Add the bacon back to the pan along with the maple syrup. Stir until the syrup is evenly coating the Brussels sprouts.

4. Season with salt and pepper and serve hot.

ROASTED RADISHES WITH BUTTER AND PARSLEY

PREP TIME: 5 minutes | COOK TIME: 20 minutes | TOTAL TIME: 25 minutes | YIELD: 3 to 4 servings

I need a bitter element in my salads, and radishes often serve that purpose when I'm using milder greens such as spinach instead of arugula. While raw radishes have a spicy kick to them, high-heat roasting mellows that bitterness to create an almost entirely new vegetable. They develop a less assertive, slightly sweet flavor. Roasted radishes are also quite juicy. While I've listed regular unsalted butter in the ingredients, this recipe would lend itself perfectly to brown butter if you have some on hand (to make your own brown butter, see page 32).

3 cups radishes, greens removed and sliced in half

1 teaspoon extra-virgin olive oil

½ teaspoon kosher salt

1 tablespoon unsalted butter, melted

1 tablespoon chopped fresh parsley

¼ teaspoon ground black pepper

1. Preheat the oven to 450° F. Line a baking sheet with aluminum foil.

2. Clean the radishes. Place in a medium bowl and toss with the oil. Spread cut side down in a single layer on the baking sheet and sprinkle with the salt. Roast until just tender, 15 to 20 minutes.

3. Place the roasted radishes on a serving plate and drizzle with butter. Top with parsley and pepper. Season with additional salt, if desired. Serve hot.

HONEY-ROASTED CARROTS WITH CUMIN

PREP TIME: 10 minutes | **COOK TIME:** 30 minutes | **TOTAL TIME:** 40 minutes | **YIELD:** 6 to 8 servings

I'm very selective about which carrots I'll buy at the store. I prefer thin carrots because they're often very sweet. Also, I think they're pretty, and presentation is important. They're authentic baby carrots, as opposed to the bagged versions that are sometimes a bit dry and lacking in flavor. However, this recipe will work with any carrot you prefer. Remember that larger carrots may require a longer roasting time.

1 pound carrots

3 tablespoons extra-virgin olive oil

3 tablespoons honey

¾ teaspoon ground cumin

½ teaspoon kosher salt, plus more for seasoning

¼ teaspoon ground black pepper, plus more for seasoning

1. Preheat the oven to 400°F. Line a baking sheet with aluminum foil.

2. Trim away the carrot greens (you may leave 1 inch of greens for presentation, if desired). Peel and place in a large bowl.

3. In a small bowl, whisk the oil, honey, cumin, salt, and pepper. Toss with the carrots until they're evenly coated.

4. Lay the carrots in a single layer on the baking sheet and drizzle any remaining liquid from the bowl on top. Roast for approximately 30 minutes, flipping halfway through, until lightly caramelized and tender. Add more salt and pepper to taste, if desired. Serve hot.

Note: For an alternate version, try cutting the honey in half to 1½ tablespoons and adding 1½ tablespoons of pure maple syrup.

KALE WITH GRAPES AND ALMONDS

PREP TIME: 10 minutes | COOK TIME: 8 minutes | TOTAL TIME: 18 minutes | YIELD: 4 to 6 servings

Have you ever sautéed or roasted grapes? It's one of the best and most innovative ways to use them, and they serve as the perfect complement to slightly bitter kale. I recommend boiling the kale for several minutes to soften it; otherwise, it will be quite chewy (baby kale is the one exception; it's very tender). Alternatively, you may massage the kale for several minutes until it darkens slightly.

5 to 6 cups kale, stems removed (approximately 1 bunch)

1 tablespoon extra-virgin olive oil

1 cup red seedless grapes, halved

1 clove garlic, minced

¼ cup toasted slivered almonds

1 teaspoon kosher salt

1. Bring a large pot of water to a boil. Add the kale, pushing it below the surface with a slotted spoon so that it cooks evenly. Cook until the kale is wilted, 2 to 3 minutes, then drain in a colander. Pat dry and set aside

2. In a large nonstick skillet, heat 1½ teaspoons of the oil over medium-high heat. Place the grapes flat-side down in the pan and sauté, gently swirling the pan to prevent sticking, until slightly caramelized, 1 to 2 minutes. Remove the grapes from the pan and set aside.

3. Add the remaining 1½ teaspoons oil to the pan and turn the heat to low. Add the garlic and cook for 1 to 2 minutes, stirring periodically, until fragrant.

4. Add the kale, almonds, grapes, and salt, stirring to combine. Serve warm.

SAUTÉED FRESH CORN WITH CHILI AND LIME

PREP TIME: 10 minutes | **COOK TIME:** 5 minutes | **TOTAL TIME:** 15 minutes | **YIELD:** 6 to 8 servings

Fresh corn sautéed with butter, salt, and pepper is a basic side dish that pairs wonderfully with many entrées. If you want to spruce it up a bit, add some spice and citrus. Try this version with dishes with a Tex-Mex or barbecue twist.

8 ears yellow or white corn
(6 to 8 cups kernels)

3 tablespoons unsalted butter

1 teaspoon kosher salt

¼ teaspoon ground black
pepper

1 teaspoon chili powder

⅛ teaspoon cayenne

1 tablespoon fresh lime juice
(approximately 1 lime)

1 serrano or jalapeño pepper,
seeded and minced (optional)

1. Remove the husks and silk from the corn, and slice off the kernels.

2. In a large Dutch oven or heavy-bottom saucepan, melt the butter over medium heat. Stir in the corn kernels, salt, black pepper, chili powder, and cayenne. Cook uncovered for approximately 5 minutes, stirring periodically, until the corn is tender and heated through.

3. Remove from the heat and stir in the lime juice and serrano pepper, if using. Serve hot.

ROASTED BABY ARTICHOKES

PREP TIME: 10 minutes | **COOK TIME:** 20 minutes | **TOTAL TIME:** 30 minutes | **YIELD:** 2 to 3 servings

In most cases, I prefer fresh produce over canned, but artichokes are often the exception. Canned artichokes taste great in recipes and they save so much time. I was a little stunned the first time I cooked with fresh artichokes. There's a lot of prep work involved (unless a pressure cooker is used, but that's for another cookbook). So most of the time I stick with canned artichokes. I will, however, make an exception for baby artichokes when they're in season. There's still some prep work involved but not nearly as much. Except for a few tough exterior leaves, the entire artichoke is edible, since the choke hasn't fully matured. When roasted, these are crispy on the outside and tender in the middle.

12 baby artichokes

1 lemon, halved, plus
1 tablespoon lemon juice

3 tablespoons extra-virgin olive oil

2 teaspoons kosher salt

¼ teaspoon ground black pepper

¼ cup freshly grated Parmigiano-Reggiano cheese

2 tablespoon chopped fresh parsley

1. Preheat the oven to 425°F. Line a baking sheet with aluminum foil.

2. Slice off the top one-third of the artichoke head and remove the tough outer leaves and stems. Use a vegetable peeler to remove the tough outer green layer from the stem. Use a knife to slice down the center, from top to stem. The artichokes will begin to oxidize immediately, so rub the exposed centers with one of the lemon halves as you work to keep them from browning (a little browning is okay since they'll caramelize in the oven).

3. In a large bowl, whisk the oil and lemon juice. Add the artichokes and toss to combine, then spread evenly on the baking sheet and drizzle with any excess oil. Sprinkle the salt and pepper evenly on top and roast for 20 minutes, or until tender.

4. Squeeze more fresh lemon juice over the artichokes and top with the cheese and parsley. Serve hot.

ROASTED BROCCOLI WITH ASIAGO, GARLIC, AND SLIVERED ALMONDS

PREP TIME: 5 minutes | **COOK TIME:** 20 minutes | **TOTAL TIME:** 25 minutes | **YIELD:** 3 to 4 servings

Roasted broccoli is one of my absolute favorite vegetable preparations. The buds on the broccoli florets become crunchy and brown, and the flavors are much more pronounced. This version is inspired by the first roasted broccoli recipe I ever tried, from Ina Garten. That recipe convinced me that roasting is almost always preferable to steaming. Take a peek at the broccoli after 15 to 20 minutes; the roasting time will vary based on how small the broccoli florets are cut. If you have trouble locating Asiago cheese, Parmesan is a great substitute.

1½ pounds broccoli, cut into small florets

3 tablespoons extra-virgin olive oil

2 to 3 cloves garlic, sliced thin

½ teaspoon kosher salt

¼ teaspoon ground black pepper

1 medium lemon, sliced in half

3 tablespoons toasted slivered almonds

¼ cup freshly grated Asiago cheese

1. Preheat the oven to 425°F and line a baking sheet with aluminum foil.

2. In a large bowl, toss the broccoli, oil, garlic, salt, and pepper (see note). Spread evenly on the pan, drizzling any excess oil on top, and roast in the oven for 20 to 25 minutes until the florets are crispy and caramelized, but still a little tender. Check the broccoli after 15 to 20 minutes.

3. Squeeze the lemon over the broccoli and top with the almonds and cheese. Serve hot.

Note: You may add more or less olive oil, lemon juice, salt, pepper, or cheese to taste.

BAKED ACORN SQUASH WITH GARLIC-YOGURT SAUCE

PREP TIME: 45 minutes (mostly inactive) | **COOK TIME:** 35 minutes
TOTAL TIME: 1 hour 20 minutes (mostly inactive) | **YIELD:** 2 to 4 servings

This recipe is inspired by an Afghan dish known as kaddo bourani. It's traditionally prepared with pumpkin, though here I replace it with acorn squash which is a naturally sweet, incredibly addicting substitute. Cinnamon and a touch of sugar balance a warm and tangy garlic-yogurt sauce for a unique dish that's savory, sweet, and perfect for cozy fall dinners. The longer the garlic and the yogurt sit together, the more pronounced the garlic flavor will be. The sauce can be prepared one or two days in advance.

¾ cup full-fat plain yogurt

1 teaspoon minced garlic

½ teaspoon kosher salt

1 large acorn squash

½ cup granulated sugar

½ teaspoon ground cinnamon

¼ teaspoon ground coriander

1 tablespoon clarified butter or vegetable oil

1. Combine the yogurt, garlic, and ¼ teaspoon of the salt. (Milk can be added to the yogurt to thin the sauce if necessary.) Set aside for at least 30 minutes.

2. Using a sharp knife, carefully slice off the ends of the acorn squash, lay flat side down, and slice through the middle. Scoop out the seeds and slice into ¾- to 1-inch strips.

3. In a small bowl, combine the sugar, cinnamon, coriander, and the remaining ¼ teaspoon salt.

4. Preheat the oven to 350°F. Heat the butter in a Dutch oven or heavy-bottom saucepan over medium to medium-high heat. Using tongs, brown the acorn squash slices well on both sides, in batches if necessary, approximately 1 minute per side. To avoid overcrowding the pan, I recommend browning half the squash at a time. Watch out for oil splatters and cover the pan if necessary.

5. Remove the pot from the heat and sprinkle the spice mixture evenly over the squash. Cover and bake for 30 minutes.

6. Remove the pot from the oven and toss the cooked squash with the glaze at the bottom of the pan. Be careful not to break apart the squash.

7. Drizzle the yogurt sauce over the squash and serve.

PARMESAN RISOTTO

PREP TIME: 15 minutes | **COOK TIME:** 2 hours 30 minutes (mostly inactive)
TOTAL TIME: 2 hours 45 minutes (mostly inactive) | **YIELD:** 6 to 8 servings

One of the first culinary books to have a big influence on me was *Zingerman's Guide to Good Eating* by Ari Weinzweig. An entire section is devoted to the wonders of Parmigiano-Reggiano and how it differs from much of the standard Parmesan cheese sold in stores today. Weinzweig points out that Parmigiano-Reggiano rinds have no wax, no coloring, and no additives; they're made simply from dried cheese. In his book, he suggests freezing leftover rinds to infuse in stocks, but it was years before I actually tried this. Rinds are available at many large grocery stores, or save your own as you go. Parmesan stock is incredibly savory, and it makes an excellent base for this risotto. The stock can be made 48 hours in advance.

FOR THE STOCK:

1 pound Parmigiano-Reggiano rinds

4 cups chicken or vegetable stock, preferably homemade (pages 15, 16)

4 cups water

FOR THE RISOTTO:

4 cups homemade Parmesan stock

1 tablespoon extra-virgin olive oil

1 cup finely diced yellow onion (approximately 1 medium)

Pinch of kosher salt

1 cup Arborio or carnaroli rice

½ cup dry white wine

¼ cup freshly grated Parmigiano-Reggiano cheese, plus more for garnish

2 tablespoons chopped fresh parsley, plus more for garnish

1. In a large Dutch oven or saucepan, bring the Parmigiano-Reggiano rinds, stock, and water to a boil. Reduce the heat to low and simmer for 2 hours, stirring periodically to prevent the rinds from sticking to the bottom of the pan. Strain, squeezing excess liquid from the rinds by pressing with a slotted spoon. Discard the rinds. This should yield approximately 4 cups Parmesan stock, though less is possible depending on liquid reduction.

2. Bring 4 cups of Parmesan stock to a gentle simmer in a medium saucepan over low heat (if less than 4 cups Parmesan stock was rendered, substitute the remaining measurement with water).

3. Add the oil to a Dutch oven or sautoir and place over medium-low heat. Add the onion and a pinch of salt, and cook until tender and translucent, 3 to 5 minutes. Add the rice to the pan and stir for approximately 1 minute. Add the wine and stir until it has evaporated.

4. Add 1 cup hot stock; simmer until absorbed, stirring periodically. Add the remaining stock ½ cup at a time, allowing it to absorb into the rice before adding more. Stir frequently until the rice is creamy and tender, 18 to 20 minutes (see note).

5. Remove from the heat and stir in the cheese and parsley. Before serving, top with additional cheese and parsley.

Note: Alternatively, you can replace Parmesan stock with 4 cups of chicken or vegetable stock, if you prefer.

OATMEAL STOUT BEER BREAD

PREP TIME: 10 minutes | **COOK TIME:** 50 minutes | **TOTAL TIME:** 1 hour | **YIELD:** 10 to 12 servings

I'm a total sucker for beer bread because it's very fast and easy to prepare. There's no kneading, no stand mixers, and no added yeast aside from what's already in the beer. Making beer bread is easier than baking muffins, which makes this a perfect recipe for beginners. Samuel Smith Oatmeal Stout Beer is a great option for this recipe because of its slightly sweet, smooth flavor. Feel free to experiment with other oatmeal stout beers; just make sure to use the same volume of liquid.

15 ounces (3 cups) all-purpose flour

½ cup old-fashioned rolled oats

¼ cup dark brown sugar

4½ teaspoons baking powder

2 teaspoons kosher salt

1 (12-ounce) bottle Samuel Smith Oatmeal Stout Beer

2 ounces (4 tablespoons) unsalted butter, melted

1. Preheat the oven to 350°F. Lightly grease a 9 x 5-inch loaf pan with baking spray or butter and place on a baking sheet.

2. In a medium bowl, whisk the flour, oats, sugar, baking powder, and salt.

3. Pour the beer into the dry ingredients and stir until just combined. The dough will be thick and sticky. Transfer to the loaf pan and gently press down. Evenly pour the butter over the top of the batter and bake until golden brown on top, 50 to 55 minutes.

4. Allow to cool, in the pan, on a rack for 15 minutes before slicing.

PUMPKIN-SPICED DINNER ROLLS

PREP TIME: 1 hour 40 minutes (mostly inactive) | **COOK TIME:** 20 minutes
TOTAL TIME: 2 hours (mostly inactive) | **YIELD:** 10 large rolls

Are you wondering what you might do with pumpkin-spiced dinner rolls? Let me offer a few suggestions. These are perfect as a side for your Thanksgiving dinner. Imagine dipping them in turkey gravy or using them to scoop up homemade stuffing. You can also slice them in half to use as buns for pulled pork or serve them with homemade chili.

⅓ cup lukewarm water

½ ounce active dry yeast (approximately 1½ tablespoons)

2 ounces (4 tablespoons) unsalted butter, melted and cooled slightly

¼ cup granulated sugar

1 cup pumpkin puree

2 large eggs, lightly beaten

½ teaspoons kosher salt

2 teaspoons pumpkin pie spice

17 ounces (4 scant cups) all-purpose flour, plus more as needed

1. In the bowl of a stand mixer, whisk the water and yeast until bubbly and allow it to sit for 1 minute. Add the butter, sugar, pumpkin puree, and eggs and whisk until just combined.

2. In a separate bowl, stir the salt and the pumpkin pie spice into the flour with a fork. Attach a dough hook to the mixer, and turn the mixer on low speed. Add the salt and flour to the liquid ingredients.

3. Allow the dough to mix for approximately 5 minutes on low speed. It should be sticky. If it's not coming together, add up to 4 more tablespoons of flour, 1 to 2 tablespoons at a time. Rub a small amount of vegetable oil on your palms to keep the dough from sticking when handling.

4. Place the dough in a lightly greased large bowl and cover with a dish towel. Allow to double in size at room temperature, approximately 1 hour.

5. Preheat the oven to 350°F and lightly grease with baking spray or butter two 8-inch cake pans. Divide the dough into 10 equal-sized balls and place 5 in each cake pan. Allow the dough to rise for another 25 to 30 minutes before placing in the oven.

6. Bake for 20 minutes or until an internal thermometer reads 190°F. Serve warm.

PUMPKIN SAGE DROP BISCUITS

PREP TIME: 10 minutes | **COOK TIME:** 15 minutes | **TOTAL TIME:** 25 minutes | **YIELD:** 19 to 24 biscuits

These drop biscuits make a fantastic fall side dish if you're serving soup or a stew. They're hot and buttery right out of the oven, but you can really taste the pumpkin and sage flavors after they've cooled for a while. They're also a great option for breakfast and brunch. I like eating them with a bit of salted butter in the morning while I sip on my coffee.

10 ounces (2 cups) all-purpose flour

1 tablespoon baking powder

¼ teaspoon baking soda

1½ teaspoons granulated sugar

1 teaspoon kosher salt

¼ teaspoon ground cinnamon

¼ teaspoon freshly grated nutmeg

2 teaspoons finely chopped fresh sage

4 ounces (8 tablespoons) unsalted butter, cold and cut into small cubes

¾ cup pumpkin puree

¾ cup buttermilk

1. Preheat the oven to 400°F and line one large or two small baking sheets with parchment paper.

2. In a large bowl, whisk the flour, baking powder, baking soda, sugar, salt, cinnamon, nutmeg, and sage.

3. Add the butter and use your fingers to work it into the dry ingredients until it resembles coarse cornmeal with a few scattered larger pieces of butter.

4. In a separate bowl, whisk the pumpkin puree and buttermilk. Pour into the dry ingredients, and use a spatula to fold together until just combined (less mixing equals softer biscuits).

5. Use an ⅛ cup (2 tablespoon) cookie scoop to portion the biscuits onto the baking sheet; place at least 2 inches apart. Bake for 15 to 17 minutes, until crisp on the outside and tender in the middle.

An ounce of sauce covers a multitude of sins.
—Anthony Bourdain

MAIN COURSES

This chapter is divided into three sections: meat and poultry, seafood, and vegetarian. There are many evenings where I opt for a salad or soup instead of a big dinner. More often than not, these are the meals I love cooking for family and friends. There are memories associated with many of these recipes. The grilled barbecued chicken is inspired by a recipe my mom made for my father because his mother prepared it for him when he was a child. The jumbo lump crab cake sliders are adapted from my grandmother's recipe. While some of these entrées are good everyday meals, many of them are also geared toward special occasions, either because they're a bit advanced or because they're slightly more decadent. If you're seeking an easy, healthy dinner, look no further than my maple soy glazed salmon. For a hearty, comforting meal, try the Andouille macaroni and cheese.

MEAT AND POULTRY

SWEET-AND-SPICY BARBECUED CHICKEN THIGHS

PREP TIME: 45 minutes | **COOK TIME:** 1 hour | **TOTAL TIME:** 1 hour 45 minutes | **YIELD:** 3 to 4 servings

When I was growing up, my mother often prepared chicken and rice with barbecue sauce for dinner. Mom's version used a bottled sauce, and she would baste boneless, skinless thighs and allow them to roast in the oven. These sweet-and-spicy chicken thighs were served over white rice with more of the sauce on top. I wanted to create a similar sauce from scratch, and I think I've done a pretty good job of replicating the flavor. I went with bone-in, skin-on chicken thighs (they're less expensive and juicier), and I let them cook low and slow on the grill. You can serve the chicken with your favorite barbecue sides, but I prefer to stick with white rice for old time's sake.

FOR THE SAUCE:

1 cup white wine vinegar

1 cup ketchup

1 tablespoon Worcestershire sauce

1 tablespoon fresh-squeezed lemon juice

2 teaspoons Frank's RedHot sauce

½ cup dark brown sugar

¼ teaspoon garlic powder

¼ teaspoon onion powder

½ tablespoon kosher salt

½ teaspoon ground black pepper

⅛ teaspoon ground cloves

⅛ teaspoon ground allspice

FOR THE CHICKEN:

8 bone-in, skin-on chicken thighs

Kosher salt

Ground black pepper

Vegetable oil, or any neutral-flavored, high-heat oil

White rice for serving (optional)

1. In a medium saucepan, whisk the vinegar, ketchup, Worcestershire, lemon juice, hot sauce, brown sugar, garlic powder, onion powder, salt, pepper, cloves, and allspice. Bring the mixture to a boil, then turn the heat down to medium-low. Allow the sauce to simmer for 15 minutes, uncovered, stirring periodically (see note).

2. Remove the chicken thighs from the fridge and allow them to come to room temperature for 30 minutes. Trim away excess skin and season the skin side liberally with salt and pepper.

3. Preheat a gas grill to medium heat. The chicken needs to cook over indirect heat. If using a grill with two burners, keep one burner turned off. If using a grill with three or four burners, keep one of the middle burners turned off. Oil the grates with a neutral, high-heat oil such as vegetable oil.

4. Pour ½ cup of barbecue sauce into a small bowl for basting (reserve the rest for serving). Place the

recipe continued on next page

chicken skin side up on the side of the grill with the indirect heat (the side where the burner is turned off) and close the lid. Cook for approximately 15 minutes, and then use tongs to turn the thighs over and cook for another 10 minutes with the lid closed. Move the thighs to the direct heat side of the grill, close the lid, and cook for 5 minutes on each side to sear the meat (10 minutes total). Baste generously with the barbecue sauce and cook for another 1 to 2 minutes, uncovered. Turn the thighs over, baste, and cook for another 1 to 2 minutes, uncovered.

5. Remove the chicken and allow it to cool briefly. Serve with the remaining sauce on top.

Note: Sauce recipe yields 1½ cups. It can be prepared up to 3 days in advance.

KOREAN BARBECUE SLOW COOKER PULLED PORK TACOS

PREP TIME: 30 minutes | **COOK TIME:** 8 hours 30 minutes (mostly inactive)
TOTAL TIME: 9 hours (mostly inactive) | **YIELD:** 15 to 20 tacos

I've always been drawn to fusion cuisines, probably because I love breaking all kitchen rules. I also think that unless I'm trying a particular cuisine in its country of origin, it's questionable as to whether I've even tried an authentic version of a particular dish. These pulled pork tacos combine elements from two of my favorite cuisines: Korean and Mexican. There are a lot of ingredients here, but the dish is easy to prepare and will make a lot of food. All of the components can be prepared in advance and will last for several days.

FOR THE PORK:
3-pound boneless pork shoulder (or 4-pound bone-in shoulder)

4 cloves garlic, peeled

1 tablespoon kosher salt

1 teaspoon ground black pepper

FOR THE BARBECUE SAUCE:
2 tablespoons seasoned rice vinegar

1 tablespoon cornstarch

1 tablespoon extra-virgin olive oil

½ cup finely diced yellow onion (approximately ½ medium)

2 cloves garlic, minced

2 tablespoons soy sauce

1½ cups chicken or vegetable stock, preferably homemade (pages 15 and 16)

⅓ cup gochujang chili paste

2 tablespoons tomato paste

2 tablespoon packed dark brown sugar

1½ teaspoons toasted sesame oil

FOR THE SLAW:
2½ cups shredded Napa cabbage

½ cup grated carrot

2 tablespoons thinly sliced scallions

3 tablespoons rice vinegar

1 tablespoon toasted sesame oil

1½ teaspoons soy sauce

ADDITIONAL INGREDIENTS FOR SERVING:
15 to 20 warm corn tortillas

Gochujang chili paste

Fresh chopped cilantro

PREPARE THE PORK:

1. Using a paring knife to make small incisions, press the garlic cloves into the pork shoulder, spacing them out to maximize the flavor infusion.

recipe continued on next page

2. Season all sides of the pork with salt and pepper. Place the pork, fat side down, in a slow cooker and cook on low heat for 8 hours, or 5 hours on high heat (cooking longer on low heat will yield a more tender cut).

3. Carefully remove the pork from the slow cooker and place in a large bowl. Use two forks to shred the meat into small pieces. Test for seasoning; if needed, drizzle with the seasoned liquid from the slow cooker or add salt and pepper to taste.

PREPARE THE SAUCE:

1. In a small bowl, whisk the vinegar and cornstarch.

2. In a large saucepan, heat the olive oil over medium-low heat. Add the onion and garlic. Sweat, stirring periodically, until translucent, approximately 5 minutes. Add the soy sauce and rice vinegar–cornstarch mixture, stock, gochujang, tomato paste, and sugar, whisking to combine. Turn the heat to high and bring the ingredients to a boil, then reduce the heat to low and simmer for 30 to 40 minutes, until the sauce has thickened.

3. Remove from the heat and stir in the sesame oil.

4. Pour the sauce into the bowl with the pork and toss to combine.

PREPARE THE SLAW:

1. In a medium bowl, toss the cabbage, carrots, and scallions.

2. In a small bowl, whisk the rice vinegar, sesame oil, and soy sauce.

3. Pour the dressing over the vegetables and toss to combine.

SERVING INSTRUCTIONS:

1. Preheat the oven to 350°F. Wrap stacks of five or fewer tortillas in aluminum foil and place in the oven until heated through, 10 to 15 minutes. Alternately, tortillas can be warmed individually in a skillet over medium-low heat.

2. Whisk the gochujang with warm water for a more spreadable, sauce-like consistency (approximately 1 tablespoon water per 2 tablespoons gochujang).

3. Top each tortilla with pulled pork, Asian slaw, a drizzle of gochujang, and cilantro.

CUMIN-MARINATED GRILLED FLANK STEAK WITH SALSA

PREP TIME: 6 hours 20 minutes (mostly inactive) | **COOK TIME:** 10 minutes
TOTAL TIME: 6 hours 30 minutes (mostly inactive) | **YIELDS:** 4 servings

Flank steak is a perfect, inexpensive cut of meat for grilling and broiling; it readily soaks up marinade flavors. The broiler is a fine alternative to the grill during the off-season (and for those without access to a grill), but it doesn't capture the same smokiness. This cumin-marinated grilled flank steak is an easy dinner that celebrates those charred smoky flavors I love so very much. You can use any brand of salsa, but bonus points if you find one that lists cumin as one of the main ingredients.

⅓ cup extra-virgin olive oil

½ cup mild or medium salsa, plus more for serving

2 tablespoons fresh-squeezed lime juice (1 to 2 limes)

1 tablespoon Worcestershire sauce

2 cloves garlic, smashed

1 teaspoon ground cumin

2 tablespoons roughly chopped fresh cilantro

½ teaspoon kosher salt, plus more for seasoning

1½ pounds flank steak, fat trimmed

Ground black pepper

1. Place the oil, salsa, lime juice, Worcestershire, garlic, cumin, cilantro, and ½ teaspoon salt in a large resealable plastic bag. Add the flank steak, seal, and toss to coat the meat with the marinade. Place the bag in a bowl, and place the bowl in the refrigerator. Marinate for a minimum of 6 hours or overnight, turning the bag periodically.

2. Remove the bowl and bag from the refrigerator and allow the steak to come to room temperature before grilling, at least 30 minutes. When you're ready to cook, preheat the grill to the highest temperature. Discard the marinade and pat the steak dry. Season both sides generously with salt and pepper.

3. Grill the steak on high heat for approximately 3 to 4 minutes per side until it's cooked to medium-rare. Remove from the heat and allow the meat to rest for at least 10 minutes. Slice against the grain into thin strips. Serve topped with additional salsa.

ANDOUILLE MACARONI AND CHEESE

PREP TIME: 5 minutes | **COOK TIME:** 25 minutes | **TOTAL TIME:** 30 minutes | **YIELD:** 4 to 6 servings

Homemade macaroni and cheese might sound intimidating at first, but it's actually easy and quick to prepare. The sauce is made from béchamel, a basic French white sauce. Though it sounds fancy, it's made from three kitchen staples: flour, butter, and milk. I like using turkey Andouille in this recipe because it's a bit leaner and the cheese sauce is already very rich. Regular Andouille will work as well, but make sure to thoroughly drain excess fat from the sausage using paper towels. Both sharp and mild cheddar cheese will work in this recipe.

1 pound dry elbow pasta

18 ounces (approximately 6 links) precooked turkey Andouille sausage, diced small

1 to 2 teaspoons extra-virgin olive oil as needed

3 ounces (6 tablespoons) unsalted butter

¼ cup plus 2 tablespoons all-purpose flour

3 cups whole milk (2% milk can be substituted)

½ teaspoon kosher salt

10 ounces cheddar cheese, grated (approximately 2¾ cups)

Ground black pepper

1. Bring a large pot of salted water to a rolling boil. Cook the pasta until al dente, 8 to 10 minutes. Drain, rinse briefly to prevent sticking, and set aside.

2. In a large nonstick skillet, cook the Andouille sausage over medium heat, stirring periodically, until brown and crispy, approximately 5 minutes. If the sausage begins sticking to the pan, add 1 to 2 teaspoons oil.

3. In a Dutch oven or large saucepan, melt the butter over medium-low heat. Add the flour, whisking to combine. Continue whisking for approximately 5 minutes. Slowly whisk in the milk, add the salt, and turn up the heat to bring the mixture to a boil, whisking constantly. The mixture will begin to thicken. Continue whisking vigorously for 2 to 5 minutes, or until the mixture is creamy and velvety, making sure to periodically scrape the bottom of the pan to prevent congealment. Remove from the heat and immediately whisk in the cheese, a handful at a time, while the sauce is still hot. Stir in the elbow pasta, coating evenly with the sauce. Season with additional salt, if desired.

4. Before serving, top each bowl of macaroni and cheese with a generous helping of sausage and pepper.

FARFALLE WITH SUN-DRIED TOMATOES, PANCETTA, AND ROQUEFORT

PREP TIME: 15 minutes | **COOK TIME:** 45 minutes | **TOTAL TIME:** 1 hour | **YIELD:** 4 to 6 servings

This is quite a rich pasta dish, so I recommend saving it for special occasions (or emergency comfort food). I prefer using sun-dried tomatoes packed in oil because they are incredibly soft and the flavor has had a chance to mellow slightly, but regular sun-dried tomatoes will work just as well. If using the latter, allow them to soak in boiling water thoroughly until they have had a chance to soften.

1 tablespoon extra-virgin olive oil

¼ cup diced pancetta

3 to 4 cloves garlic, minced

½ cup chicken stock, preferably homemade (page 15)

½ cup heavy cream

½ cup sun-dried tomatoes in oil, drained and sliced thin

1 pound dry farfalle pasta

½ cup crumbled Roquefort cheese

½ cup chopped or thinly sliced fresh basil

¼ cup toasted pine nuts

1. In a saucepan, heat the oil over medium-low heat and add the pancetta. Allow the pancetta to cook, stirring periodically, until crispy and caramelized. Use a slotted spoon or spatula to remove from the saucepan and place on a plate lined with paper towels. Set aside.

2. Turn the heat down to low. Add the garlic and allow to cook until fragrant, approximately 1 minute. Whisk in the chicken stock and heavy cream, followed by the sun-dried tomatoes. It is normal for the oil and cream to separate. Turn the heat up to medium and allow the sauce to reduce until thickened, 5 to 10 minutes.

3. While the sauce is reducing, bring a large pot of water to a boil. Cook the farfalle until al dente, 8 to 10 minutes. Drain and set aside.

4. Remove the sauce from the heat and stir in the Roquefort until well blended. Toss the sauce with the pasta. Top with basil, pine nuts, and the reserved pancetta before serving.

PISTACHIO-CRUSTED PORK TENDERLOIN WITH CHERRY RHUBARB COMPOTE

PREP TIME: 20 minutes | **COOK TIME:** 40 minutes | **TOTAL TIME:** 1 hour | **YIELD:** 6 to 8 servings

When I began to learn how to cook as an adult (that's still embarrassing to write), one of the first recipes I attempted was a pork tenderloin dish. It turned into a comedy of errors that I try to remember when writing recipes today. Common sense in the kitchen often comes from experience, and little tips and tricks that are obvious to me now led to a kitchen full of smoke back then. One of the things I wish I knew when first working with pork: use a thermometer when preparing tenderloins, because the cooking time will vary depending on the size and weight of the meat.

FOR THE CHERRY RHUBARB COMPOTE:

1 tablespoon extra-virgin olive oil

½ cup diced yellow onion (approximately 1 small)

Pinch of kosher salt

2 cups sweet cherries, pitted and chopped

1 cup thinly sliced rhubarb (approximately 1 to 2 stalks)

¼ cup fresh-squeezed orange juice

FOR THE PORK:

½ cup panko bread crumbs

½ cup finely chopped pistachios

½ teaspoon finely chopped fresh thyme leaves

½ teaspoon kosher salt

½ teaspoon ground black pepper

1 large egg white, lightly beaten

1 pound pork tenderloin

PREPARE THE COMPOTE:

1. In a medium saucepan, heat the oil over medium-low heat. Add the onion along with a pinch of salt and cook until translucent, stirring periodically, 3 to 5 minutes.

2. Add the cherries, rhubarb, and orange juice and turn the heat up to medium. Once simmering, reduce the heat slightly and mash the fruit, retaining a bit of texture. Continue cooking, stirring periodically, for an additional 7 to 10 minutes, or until the rhubarb is tender.

PREPARE THE PORK:

1. Preheat the oven to 375°F and line a baking sheet with aluminum foil.

2. Combine the bread crumbs, pistachios, thyme, salt, and pepper in a large casserole dish. Whisk the egg white in a small bowl.

3. Pat the tenderloin dry with paper towels. Brush the tenderloin with the egg white and dredge thoroughly in the pistachio mixture. Place on the baking sheet and press any leftover topping onto the meat to help it adhere.

4. Bake until the center of the tenderloin reaches an internal temperature of 140°F, 25 to 30 minutes. Allow the meat to rest for at least 10 minutes.

5. Slice and serve with the compote.

SEARED DUCK BREAST
WITH MACERATED CHERRIES

PREP TIME: 45 minutes | **COOK TIME:** 15 minutes | **TOTAL TIME:** 1 hour | **YIELD:** 4 servings

Until recently, it was not common to find duck meat for sale at local grocery stores. I've been so pleased to see it becoming more available recently because it's a truly satisfying dinner. It takes very little effort to feel like I'm having an upscale restaurant meal, when in truth there's only the slightest bit more effort than if I was pan-searing chicken thighs. With duck breasts, you want to score the fat all the way through without cutting into the meat. Then you slowly render most of that fat before turning up the heat and getting it nice and crispy. I always store the leftover duck fat. Keep it in the refrigerator and use it to sauté eggs or vegetables, or pan-fry potatoes. It's good stuff.

2 cups sour cherries, pitted (sweet cherries may be substituted)

2 teaspoons granulated sugar

2 teaspoons Kirsch cherry brandy

4 duck breasts

Kosher salt

Ground black pepper

1. In a medium bowl, stir the cherries, sugar, and Kirsch. Cover and place in the refrigerator for at least 30 minutes, stirring once or twice.

2. Preheat the oven to 400°F. Using a sharp knife, score the duck fat with diagonal crisscross slashes, approximately ½ inch apart, to make a diamond pattern, being careful not to cut through to the meat. Season generously with salt and pepper.

3. Place the duck breasts in a large sauté pan, skin side down (don't overcrowd the pan; cook in two batches if necessary). Place the sauté pan on the stove and turn the heat to low. Slowly turn the heat up to medium-low and allow the fat to render. Once most of the fat has cooked down, which should take approximately 10 minutes, turn the heat up to medium and sear until brown and crispy. Use tongs to turn the breasts over and sear for another minute. Turn the breasts back to skin side down and place the pan in the oven until an internal thermometer reads 130°F. Allow the meat to rest for at least 5 minutes and then slice on the bias.

4. To serve, spoon the macerated cherries along with some of their juices on top of the duck.

SPICY GOCHUJANG CHICKEN WINGS

PREP TIME: 10 minutes | COOK TIME: 1 hour | TOTAL TIME: 1 hour 10 minutes | YIELD: 4 servings

Korean fried chicken has become one of my favorite guilty pleasures. Nothing quite beats ordering wings fried at a restaurant, but I've created an easy home version. To simplify things, I broil the wings instead of deep-frying them. Gochujang is the key ingredient—a Korean chili paste that's both sweet and spicy. Every broiler is slightly different, so watch the wings during the final stages of cooking, to make sure they don't go from caramelized to burned.

Approximately 3 pounds chicken wings

¼ cup plus 2 tablespoons extra-virgin olive oil

½ teaspoon kosher salt

¾ cup gochujang chili paste

2 tablespoons water

1. Preheat the oven to 400°F. Line a baking sheet with aluminum foil.

2. Place the chicken wings in a large bowl along with the ¼ cup oil. Toss to coat evenly and spread the wings in a single layer on the baking sheet.

3. Sprinkle with the salt and roast for 50 minutes.

4. While the wings are roasting, whisk the gochujang, the 2 tablespoons oil, and the water in a medium bowl.

5. When the wings finish cooking, remove them from the oven and turn on the broiler to low. Carefully place an oven rack on one of the top shelves. Use a pastry brush to generously baste the wings with the sauce and drizzle any remaining sauce over the top. Broil for 5 to 10 minutes, until the sauce is cooked on and slightly charring (do not overbroil, as the sauce can burn easily).

SEAFOOD

JUMBO LUMP CRAB CAKE SLIDERS

PREP TIME: 15 minutes | **COOK TIME:** 15 minutes | **TOTAL TIME:** 30 minutes
YIELD: approximately 7 sliders

These sliders are adapted from my grandmother's recipe. I gave up ordering crab cakes at restaurants years ago because they're never good enough for me. Zelda's crab cakes are the best, as far as I'm concerned. This is basically her recipe; I have simply made the cakes a bit smaller and refined the spice quantities to indicate ⅛ teaspoon where she calls for "a few shakes." I was lucky enough to grow up in Maryland where there is no shortage of good-quality jumbo lump crabmeat. If Maryland crabmeat is not available, I've heard Louisiana crab is an excellent substitute. If at all possible, I really do recommend using jumbo lump crabmeat. It makes a big difference.

1 pound fresh jumbo lump crab meat

½ cup Italian bread crumbs

1 teaspoon Old Bay Seasoning

⅛ teaspoon fines herbes

⅛ teaspoon garlic powder

½ teaspoon Dijon mustard

1 teaspoon Worcestershire sauce

1 large egg

½ cup mayonnaise

1 to 2 tablespoons unsalted butter

Slider buns, lightly buttered and toasted

Dijon mustard for serving (optional)

1. Place an oven rack on one of the top shelves. Line a baking sheet with aluminum foil and grease lightly with butter or cooking spray.

2. In a medium bowl, gently sort through the crabmeat to remove any shell, taking care not to break up the lumps. Add the bread crumbs, Old Bay, fines herbes, garlic powder, mustard, and Worcestershire, stirring until well combined.

3. Beat the egg in a separate bowl, and whisk in the mayonnaise until well combined.

4. A little bit at a time, gently fold the wet mixture into the crabmeat. This part takes some patience, because you really want to avoid breaking up the lumps of crab.

5. Using a kitchen scale, weigh out 7 sliders (approximately 3 ounces each). Depending on the size of the buns, you may want to increase or decrease the size.

recipe continued on next page

6. Preheat the broiler to low. Place the crab cakes on the baking sheet and top each with a small pat of butter.

7. Broil for 10 to 15 minutes, watching the crab cakes closely to make sure they don't burn. Do not flip the cakes; if the tops seem like they may be starting to burn, lower the oven rack.

8. When the tops are golden brown, remove the pan from the oven and allow the crab cakes to cool slightly before serving.

9. Serve on slider buns, with Dijon mustard, if using.

SHRIMP AND CHORIZO WITH POLENTA

PREP TIME: 10 minutes | **COOK TIME:** 40 minutes | **TOTAL TIME:** 50 minutes | **YIELD:** 4 to 6 servings

Most grocery stores sell both raw and precooked sausages. Unless I plan to remove the sausage from its casing (for example, to use in meat loaf), I almost always purchase precooked sausage to save time. You can throw it on the grill to serve on hot dog buns. Or, as I often do, you can dice or slice the sausage, get it nice and crispy in a hot pan, and add it to numerous recipes. Chorizo adds meatiness and spice to this twist on shrimp and grits. I recommend purchasing frozen shrimp that are already peeled and deveined, which is another time saver. A lot of the "fresh" shrimp sold at seafood counters has already been frozen once. It's fine to purchase thawed shrimp, but make sure to cook it within a day or two. I have specified medium shrimp, but you can use small or large shrimp depending on your preference. Just note that the cooking time will change depending on the size. For the polenta, you can use whatever milk you prefer in terms of fat content. The butter will add plenty of richness, so whole milk might be overly rich for some.

FOR THE POLENTA:

2 cups chicken stock, preferably homemade (page 15)

1 cup water

1 cup milk (1%, 2%, or whole, depending on preferred richness)

½ teaspoon kosher salt

¼ teaspoon ground black pepper

1 cup yellow cornmeal

3 tablespoons unsalted butter

FOR THE SHRIMP AND CHORIZO:

2 tablespoons extra-virgin olive oil

1½ teaspoon paprika

1 teaspoon ground coriander

¼ teaspoon ground cumin

¼ teaspoon kosher salt

4 links fully cooked chorizo (approximately 12 ounces), cut into ½ inch slices

2 cloves garlic, minced

½ cup water or chicken stock for deglazing

1 pound uncooked medium shrimp, peeled and deveined

Chopped fresh cilantro for garnish (optional)

1. To prepare the polenta, in a Dutch oven or large heavy-bottom saucepan, bring the stock, water, milk, salt, and pepper to a boil over high heat.

recipe continued on next page

2. Slowly whisk in the cornmeal and reduce the heat to low. Simmer uncovered, stirring frequently, for 30 minutes.

3. While the polenta is cooking, prepare the chorizo and shrimp. In a large saucepan, heat the oil over medium heat and add the paprika, coriander, cumin, and salt. Once the spices are fragrant, add the chorizo. Brown over high heat for several minutes. Remove from the pan and set aside.

4. If the pan seems dry, add a bit more oil to the pan to prevent sticking and burning. Add the garlic and cook for approximately 1 minute, stirring frequently.

5. Pour the water or stock into the pan to deglaze, using a spatula to scrape up and stir any brown residue at the bottom of the pan. After the liquid has reduced slightly, add the shrimp. Cook for approximately 2 minutes per side, or until pink and opaque. Remove the pan from the heat and add the cooked chorizo, stirring to incorporate. Set aside until ready to eat.

6. When the polenta has finished cooking, turn off the heat and stir in the butter. Taste for seasoning, and add more salt or pepper, if desired.

7. Serve the bowls of the polenta topped with the chorizo and shrimp. Top with cilantro, if desired.

SMOKED SALMON AND AVOCADO TARTINE

PREP TIME: 5 minutes | **COOK TIME:** 15 minutes | **TOTAL TIME:** 20 minutes | **YIELD:** 2 to 4 servings

This is an easy, simple open-faced sandwich, one that I often have for lunch on weekdays. I typically cut the recipe in half because the ingredients taste best when the bread is straight from the oven and the layers are freshly put together. It's full of protein and healthy fats. I feel satisfied and full of energy after eating this. It's everything I love in a sandwich.

2 slices naan bread

2 to 3 teaspoons extra-virgin olive oil

1 ripe avocado, pitted and sliced

Kosher salt to taste

4 to 6 ounces good-quality smoked salmon

2 tablespoons capers or more as needed

2 tablespoons chopped fresh dill

1. Preheat the oven to 350°F. Line a baking sheet with aluminum foil. Brush each piece of naan with approximately 1 teaspoon of the oil.

2. Toast in the oven for 10 to 15 minutes, or until lightly browned and crisp.

3. Layer the avocado slices evenly across the bread. Add a light sprinkling of salt on top.

4. Layer the smoked salmon on top of the avocado. Brush lightly with more oil.

5. Top with the capers and dill, and serve immediately.

BROILED TURBOT WITH WARM TOMATO RELISH

PREP TIME: 15 minutes | COOK TIME: 15 minutes | TOTAL TIME: 30 minutes | YIELD: 5 servings

Turbot is an incredibly delicate white fish, one that needs very little preparation; it can often be prepared in under ten minutes. Please note: part of this recipe requires olive oil (as opposed to extra-virgin olive oil), as it has a higher smoke point and will not burn under the broiler. Other high-heat oils, such as canola or vegetable, may be substituted during this step. The warm tomato relish is a rich accompaniment that adds color to the plate and bursts with flavor.

FOR THE WARM TOMATO RELISH:

2 tablespoons extra-virgin olive oil

¼ teaspoon kosher salt

⅛ teaspoon ground black pepper

½ cup finely chopped red onion (approximately ½ medium)

1 clove garlic, minced

1½ cups halved grape tomatoes

2 tablespoons fresh-squeezed lemon juice

1 jalapeño pepper, seeded and finely chopped (optional)

2 tablespoons chopped fresh parsley

FOR THE BROILED TURBOT:

5 (6-ounce) turbot fillets

1 tablespoon olive oil (other high-heat oils such as vegetable may be substituted)

1. In a medium saucepan or sautoir, heat the extra-virgin olive oil over low heat. Add the salt, pepper, onion, and garlic. Allow the onion and garlic to sweat for several minutes, until translucent, stirring periodically.

2. Stir in the tomatoes, 1 tablespoon of the lemon juice, and the jalapeño, if using, and cook for several more minutes, until the tomatoes have softened. Remove from the heat and stir in the parsley.

3. Place an oven rack on one of the top shelves and preheat the broiler on low. Line a baking sheet with aluminum foil and lightly grease, using cooking spray or olive oil; place the fillet on it.

4. In a small bowl, whisk the remaining 1 tablespoon lemon juice and 1 tablespoon regular olive oil and brush on top of the fillets. Sprinkle with salt and pepper.

5. Broil the turbot for 6 to 8 minutes on low, until the fish is white and flaky and the top has browned slightly. During the last minute, you may choose to turn the broiler up to high to caramelize the tops. Keep a close eye on the fillets to make sure they don't burn.

6. Serve with the warm tomato relish (briefly heat the relish just before serving if it has cooled).

MAPLE SOY GLAZED SALMON

PREP TIME: 1 hour (mostly inactive) | **COOK TIME:** 10 minutes
TOTAL TIME: 1 hour 10 minutes (mostly inactive) | **YIELD:** 4 servings

As with filleted fish in general, I'm extremely picky about salmon. Restaurant salmon is often overcooked. I've found that ten minutes in the oven on high heat yields perfect, tender, buttery fish. This marinade is my absolute favorite, and it's an easy dinner to prepare, with only five ingredients. You may omit the Sriracha, but it adds a nice touch of heat and acidity.

¼ cup pure maple syrup

3 tablespoons soy sauce

1 tablespoon Sriracha hot sauce

1 clove garlic, smashed

4 (6 to 8 ounce) salmon fillets, preferably a fattier cut

1. In a small bowl, whisk the maple syrup, soy sauce, and Sriracha. Pour into a resealable plastic bag and add the garlic and salmon fillets. Seal the bag and turn over a few times to coat the fish in the marinade. Place the bag in a bowl and marinate for 45 to 60 minutes in the refrigerator.

2. Preheat the oven to 425°F and lightly grease a baking sheet with cooking spray or extra-virgin olive oil. Remove the fish from the marinade and gently pat dry with paper towels. Pour the remaining marinade into a small saucepan and set aside. Place the fish on the baking sheet and bake for 8 to 10 minutes, or until just barely cooked through (it's better to undercook than overcook salmon).

3. While the fish is cooking, bring the marinade to a simmer over medium heat and allow it to reduce and thicken into a glaze.

4. Brush the marinade on the salmon before serving.

TUNA, AVOCADO, AND RICE BOWL

PREP TIME: 45 minutes (mostly inactive) | **COOK TIME:** 25 minutes
TOTAL TIME: 1 hour 10 minutes (mostly inactive) | **YIELD:** 2 servings

I love sushi. I try not to be a food snob, but this is one instance where I can't help myself. When we traveled around Japan in 2009, I was so spoiled by the variety and abundance of sushi-grade fish. I'm lucky to live in a city with some superb sushi restaurants, but it's not economical for us to visit them frequently. I discovered a nearby Japanese market that has excellent quality sushi-grade fish, and I can prepare it at home for a fraction of what we would spend to dine out. I don't have the patience (or skill) to create beautiful rolls or nigiri, so I prepare sushi bowls. They're so easy it almost feels like a recipe cheat. If you can find a market that sells the fish, this is a healthy and simple meal. If you're unsure where to purchase sushi-grade fish, try asking at your local Japanese restaurant.

1 cup premium short-grain white rice

1 cup water

2 teaspoons seasoned rice vinegar

8 ounces sushi-grade tuna (salmon or yellowtail may be substituted)

1 tablespoon soy sauce

1 tablespoon toasted sesame oil

1 scallion, sliced thin

⅛ teaspoon black sesame seeds

½ avocado, pitted and sliced

Nori strips (optional)

Wasabi (optional)

1. Place the rice in a colander and briefly rinse. Place in a medium saucepan with the water and bring to a boil. Reduce the heat to low, cover, and simmer for 20 minutes, or until the water is absorbed. Remove from the heat and let stand, covered, for 10 minutes. Stir in the vinegar and allow the rice to cool to room temperature.

2. While the rice is simmering, use a sharp knife and slice the tuna into 1-inch cubes. Place in a medium bowl and toss with the soy sauce and oil. Cover with plastic wrap and place in the refrigerator to marinate for at least 30 minutes.

3. Divide the rice into two bowls and top with the tuna, drizzling a bit of the extra marinade on top. Top each bowl with the scallion, sesame seeds, and avocado. Serve with nori strips and wasabi, if using.

JUMBO LUMP CRAB POT PIE

PREP TIME: 20 minutes | **COOK TIME:** 40 minutes | **TOTAL TIME:** 1 hour | **YIELD:** 4 servings

As a native Marylander, I take crabmeat seriously. When I was younger, I loved going out for steamed crabs, but these days I'd much rather have a dish that's full of jumbo lump meat. I love the instant gratification of crab cakes and crab soup. While I'm pretty insistent that crab cakes be made from jumbo lump meat, I'm a little more flexible with this recipe. You can get away with regular crabmeat. But if jumbo lump is available, it's worth it. If you have a favorite pie dough recipe, you can use it in place of the puff pastry. Adjust the oven to the same temperature you would normally use to cook the pie dough. Delectable and flaky crabmeat meets traditional, buttery pot pie in this recipe that will both comfort and impress.

1 pound fresh jumbo lump crabmeat

4 ounces (8 tablespoons) unsalted butter

2 cups finely chopped yellow onion (approximately 1 large)

¾ cup finely chopped celery (approximately 3 ribs)

2 cloves garlic, minced

½ cup all-purpose flour

1 tablespoon brandy

2½ cups seafood stock, homemade if possible (page 17)

2 teaspoons Old Bay Seasoning

¼ cup heavy cream

Kernels from 2 ears sweet corn (approximately 1 cup)

¼ cup packed flat-leaf parsley, finely chopped

1 sheet puff pastry, chilled

1 large egg, lightly beaten

1. In a small bowl, gently sort through the crabmeat to remove any shell, taking care not to break up the lumps. Set aside.

2. In a large Dutch oven or heavy-bottom saucepan, melt the butter over medium-low heat and add the onion and celery, cooking for 5 to 7 minutes until soft. Add the garlic and cook for an additional minute, stirring periodically. Slowly add the flour and cook for 3 to 4 minutes. Stir in the brandy, seafood stock, and Old Bay. Bring to a simmer and allow the sauce to thicken, stirring periodically, for 3 to 5 minutes. Stir in the heavy cream and remove from the heat. Stir in the crabmeat, corn kernels, and parsley.

3. Preheat the oven to 425°F. Divide the filling into 4 soufflé-sized ramekins (approximately 4 x 2 inches) and place on a baking sheet.

4. On a lightly floured surface, roll the puff pastry thin and cut 4 rounds ½ to 1 inch larger than the width of the ramekins.

recipe continued on next page

5. Brush the egg wash on the rim of each ramekin and ½ inch down the outer sides. Top with the puff pastry, folding the excess over and gently pressing it against the ramekins (a fork can also be lightly pressed against the pastry to help seal it to the dish). Brush the top of the dough with a light coating of egg wash, and use a small knife to poke 3 small holes in the top of each pot pie. This will help vent steam while cooking.

6. Bake for 20 to 25 minutes, or until the tops are golden brown. Allow to cool briefly before serving.

VEGETARIAN

ASPARAGUS AND SUN-DRIED TOMATO LASAGNA

PREP TIME: 10 minutes | **COOK TIME:** 50 minutes | **TOTAL TIME:** 1 hour | **YIELD:** 12 to 15 servings

When I was in college, my roommate gave me a vegetarian cookbook as a birthday gift, and in it was a recipe for asparagus lasagna. It was one of the first dishes I prepared for friends, and ever since then, the warmth of feeding loved ones has stuck with me and influenced many a recipe—this one included.

1 cup sun-dried tomatoes

2 cups water

12 dry lasagna noodles

4 cups asparagus cut in 1-inch pieces, tough ends removed, plus 3 whole asparagus for garnish

15 ounces full-fat or part-skim ricotta cheese

1½ tablespoons fresh-squeezed lemon juice (approximately 1 lemon)

3 tablespoons chopped fresh basil

2 tablespoons chopped fresh parsley

1 teaspoon kosher salt

½ teaspoon ground black pepper

4 ounces (8 tablespoons) unsalted butter

2½ ounces (½ cup) all-purpose flour

2 cups whole or 2% milk

½ cup dry white wine

¼ teaspoon freshly ground nutmeg

1¾ cups freshly grated mild cheddar cheese

Olive oil for coating

1 cup freshly grated Parmigiano-Reggiano

½ teaspoon paprika

1. Place the sun-dried tomatoes in a heatproof bowl. Bring the water to a boil, pour over the tomatoes, and let soak for 10 to 15 minutes, until soft. Drain, dice, and set aside.

2. Bring a large pot of salted water to a boil and cook the lasagna noodles until al dente, 8 to 10 minutes. Drain and rinse with cold water, taking care not to break the noodles.

3. Prepare the asparagus one of two ways: steam until just tender in a vegetable steamer, or blanch. To blanch, fill a medium bowl with ice water and set aside. Bring a pot of water to a boil, and then add the asparagus. Let cook for 1 minute. Remove the asparagus with a slotted spoon and place in the ice bath to halt the cooking process.

recipe continued on next page

4. In a large bowl, combine the ricotta, sun-dried tomatoes, asparagus, lemon juice, basil, parsley, ½ teaspoon of the salt, and ¼ teaspoon pepper. Set aside.

5. In a medium saucepan, melt the butter over low heat, and then whisk in the flour. Whisk for 2 to 3 minutes until a nutty aroma develops. Add the milk and wine, and turn the heat up to medium-high. Continue whisking until the sauce has thickened, 5 to 7 minutes. Remove from the heat and whisk in the remaining ½ teaspoon salt and ¼ teaspoon pepper along with the nutmeg and cheddar cheese.

6. Preheat the oven to 400°F and lightly grease a 9 x 13-inch pan with olive oil. Ladle a small amount of the white sauce into the bottom of the pan and spread evenly with a spatula. Top with 3 noodles, each overlapping slightly. Top with one-third of the asparagus-ricotta mixture, followed by ⅓ cup Parmigiano-Reggiano, spreading each evenly. Repeat this process once more. For the final layer, begin with a thin layer of sauce followed by 3 noodles and the remaining asparagus-ricotta mixture. Top with 3 more noodles, the remaining sauce, and the remaining Parmigiano-Reggiano. Sprinkle paprika evenly over the Parmigiano-Reggiano and garnish with the reserved asparagus.

7. Bake for 25 to 30 minutes, until the edges are golden brown. Allow the lasagna to set for at least 10 minutes before slicing.

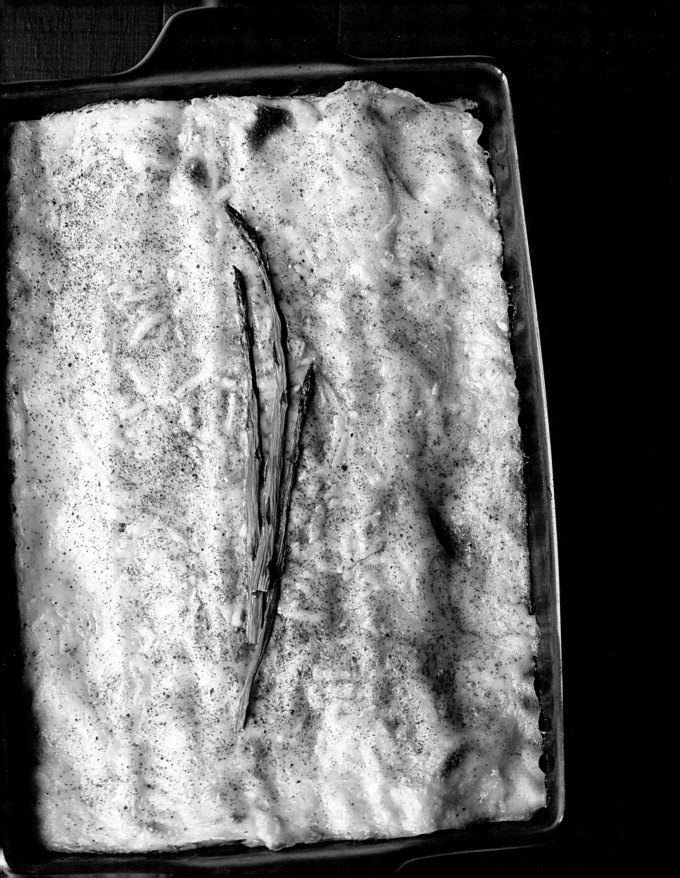

LINGUINE WITH LEMON, CRUSHED RED PEPPER, BASIL, AND BURRATA

PREP TIME: 5 minutes | COOK TIME: 15 minutes | TOTAL TIME: 20 minutes | YIELD: 4 to 6 servings

Burrata is everything I love in a cheese: it's creamy, savory, and aromatic. If finding burrata cheese is difficult, fresh mozzarella is an excellent substitute in this recipe. Crushed red peppers give this dish a spicy kick (omit if you're after a milder dish).

1 pound dry linguine

3 tablespoons extra-virgin olive oil

1 clove garlic, minced

1 teaspoon crushed red pepper flakes

3 tablespoons fresh-squeezed lemon juice (approximately 1 lemon)

½ teaspoon grated lemon zest

¼ cup thinly sliced fresh basil

½ teaspoon kosher salt

Approximately 8 ounces burrata cheese, room temperature

Italian bread crumbs

1. Bring a large pot of salted water to a boil and cook the linguine until al dente, 8 to 10 minutes. Drain, reserving ½ cup of the pasta water, and place the pasta in a large bowl.

2. While the linguine is cooking, heat the oil in a small sauté pan over low heat. Add the garlic and red pepper flakes. Gently simmer for approximately 5 minutes, or until the garlic is fragrant.

3. Add the oil, garlic, and red pepper flakes to the pasta along with the lemon juice, lemon zest, basil, and salt. Use tongs to toss the ingredients together, adding more pasta water as needed until the mixture is evenly combined.

4. Divide the pasta among serving bowls and top each with 1½ to 2 ounces of the burrata cheese and a light sprinkling of bread crumbs.

SWEET-AND-SPICY ASIAN TOFU OVER WILTED SPINACH

PREP TIME: 1 hour 5 minutes (mostly inactive) | COOK TIME: 15 minutes
TOTAL TIME: 1 hour 20 minutes (mostly inactive) | YIELD: 2 to 4 servings

Marinated, crispy tofu is a fast, high-protein meal that is also very economical. It reminds me of pan-fried cheese but without the guilt. This recipe is excellent for lunch or dinner. The wilted spinach is really just a serving suggestion; I've also served this exact tofu preparation over rice.

1 (14-ounce) block extra-firm tofu

2 tablespoons toasted sesame oil

1 tablespoon seasoned rice vinegar

2 tablespoons soy sauce

⅓ cup sweet chili sauce, such as Mae Ploy

2 tablespoons Sriracha hot sauce

1 to 2 tablespoons vegetable oil (or any neutral high-heat oil)

6 to 8 cups fresh spinach

Kosher salt

Ground black pepper

1. Line a plate with paper towels and place the tofu on top. Set another plate over the tofu and weight it down with something heavy, like a large can or book. Let sit for 30 minutes. Slice the tofu in half lengthwise and then again diagonally, yielding 4 triangles.

2. In a small bowl, whisk the sesame oil, vinegar, and 1 tablespoon of the soy sauce. Pour into a resealable plastic bag and add the tofu, turning the bag a few times to coat evenly. Refrigerate for 30 minutes.

3. In the meantime, whisk the chili sauce, Sriracha, and the remaining tablespoon of soy sauce in another bowl. Set aside.

4. Remove the tofu from the marinade and gently pat dry to remove some excess liquid.

5. Add 1 tablespoon vegetable oil to a large skillet over medium heat. When the oil is hot, add the tofu to the pan and cook for 2 to 3 minutes per side (if the pan seems dry, add an additional tablespoon of oil before carefully flipping the tofu). Remove the tofu to a cooling rack or plate.

6. In a large nonstick skillet or Dutch oven, heat the spinach over medium-low heat with 1 tablespoon of water and a pinch of salt and pepper. Cover and allow the spinach to steam for several minutes, stirring periodically, until it has wilted and darkened in color. Serve with the tofu.

MARINATED PORTOBELLO MUSHROOM SANDWICH

PREP TIME: 40 minutes | **COOK TIME:** 20 minutes | **TOTAL TIME:** 1 hour | **YIELD:** 4 servings

Years ago, my friends and I visited a regional business called Let's Dish, where we would pay to prepare individually portioned freezer meals. They would set out recipes and raw ingredients, and we'd prep and label enough meals to last for weeks. It was a great concept, and it opened my eyes to how easy it was to cook meals from scratch. After we paid for the service a few times, I began to do the same in my home. Storing individual portions of uncooked mushrooms and buttery rolls in the freezer makes for a delicious, time-saving meal later. The mushrooms can be marinated up to 48 hours in advance.

12 ounces portobello mushrooms (approximately 3 large)

⅓ cup extra-virgin olive oil

¼ cup balsamic vinegar

2 cloves garlic, minced

1 cup diced yellow onion (approximately ½ medium)

4 ciabatta rolls (or sandwich roll of your choice)

¼ cup sun-dried tomatoes packed in oil, drained, patted dry, and sliced thin

¼ cup thinly sliced fresh basil

¼ cup crumbled feta cheese

1. Wipe the mushrooms clean with a damp paper towel and cut into ½-inch slices. Place in a large resealable plastic bag along with the oil, vinegar, garlic, and onion. Marinate in the refrigerator for at least 30 minutes and up to 48 hours.

2. Preheat the oven to 350°F. Slice the rolls in half and place on a baking sheet.

3. In a large skillet over low to medium-low heat, cook the mushrooms, onion, garlic, and marinade liquid for approximately 15 minutes, stirring occasionally, until the mushrooms are soft and the liquid has reduced.

4. Toast the rolls in the oven until warm and crisp, 5 to 7 minutes.

5. Divide the mushroom mixture evenly onto the rolls and top each with 1 tablespoon of sun-dried tomatoes, basil, and feta cheese.

BLACK BEAN TORTILLA CASSEROLE

PREP TIME: 15 minutes | **COOK TIME:** 30 minutes | **TOTAL TIME:** 45 minutes | **YIELD:** 12 to 15 servings

I sampled this Mexican tortilla casserole at an event held by the bloggers from *Three Many Cooks*, and I was absolutely smitten. It turns out their recipe was adapted from *The Mom 100 Cookbook* by Katie Workman. I have been making variations of this casserole ever since because it's fast, easy, and freezes and reheats very well. While this version follows the format of the original recipe, I've customized the ingredients to suit the taste preferences in our home.

1 tablespoon extra-virgin olive oil

2 cups coarsely chopped yellow onion (approximately ½ large)

2 medium cloves garlic, minced

1 teaspoon ground cumin

1 (14-ounce) can diced tomatoes, drained

¼ cup tomato paste

¼ cup vegetable stock, preferably homemade (page 16)

2 (15½-ounce) cans black beans, drained

1 cup poblano peppers, diced small (approximately 2 large)

Kernels from 2 ears corn (1 to 2 cups)

3 cups coarsely chopped spinach

¼ cup coarsely chopped fresh cilantro

1 teaspoon kosher salt

¼ teaspoon ground black pepper

8 corn tortillas

1½ cups grated sharp cheddar cheese

1 cup crumbled queso fresco cheese

Salsa, sour cream, guacamole (optional)

1. Preheat the oven to 400°F and lightly grease a casserole dish (approximately 8 x 11 inches) using cooking spray or olive oil.

2. Heat the oil in a large skillet over medium-low heat and add the onion and garlic. Stir for 3 to 5 minutes, or until the onion is soft. Stir in the cumin, tomatoes, tomato paste, stock, beans, peppers, corn kernels, and spinach. Cook for another 1 to 2 minutes, stirring, until the spinach has wilted. Add the cilantro, salt, and the black pepper, and remove from heat.

3. Place 2 corn tortillas in the bottom of the casserole dish and top with one-quarter of the bean-and-vegetable mixture, spreading evenly. Sprinkle ½ cup cheddar cheese on top. Repeat the layering process with the remaining ingredients. Sprinkle the queso fresco cheese on top of the casserole.

4. Bake for approximately 20 minutes or until the casserole has cooked through. Allow to cool for 5 minutes before serving. Serve with the salsa, sour cream, and guacamole, if using.

KALE, CHICKPEA, AND SWEET POTATO CURRY

PREP TIME: 10 minutes | **COOK TIME:** 20 minutes | **TOTAL TIME:** 30 minutes | **YIELD:** 5 to 6 servings

This is a hearty stew that I often prepare during fall and winter. Chickpeas, kale, and sweet potatoes play off one another with contrasting textures and harmonious flavors, brought together with rich coconut milk and spicy curry paste. There is a wide assortment of curry pastes available that vary in terms of heat level and flavor profiles; any of them will work in this recipe. One of the more common varieties I see is Thai red curry paste. That will certainly work. However, my favorite is massaman curry, a paste with a sweet, nutty flavor. You can find curry pastes in the international aisle at most grocery stores.

1 tablespoon coconut oil

1½ cups diced yellow onion (approximately 1 medium)

2 cloves garlic, minced

3 tablespoons curry paste

1 (13½-ounce) can coconut milk

1½ pounds sweet potatoes, peeled and cut into ½-inch dice (approximately 3 medium)

5 cups kale, stems removed, torn into small pieces (approximately 1 bunch)

One 15-ounce can chickpeas, drained

1 tablespoon fresh-squeezed lime juice (approximately 1 lime)

2 tablespoons chopped fresh cilantro

¼ teaspoon kosher salt (optional)

1. Melt the oil in a large Dutch oven or heavy-bottom saucepan over medium heat. Add the onion and garlic; cook for 3 to 5 minutes, until soft, stirring frequently to keep the garlic from burning.

2. Stir in the curry paste, coconut milk, and sweet potatoes. Reduce the heat to low and cover. Allow the sweet potatoes to simmer for 10 minutes, or until they are tender but not mushy, stirring periodically to prevent sticking.

3. Stir in the kale, cover, and cook for several minutes until the kale is soft and wilted. Remove from the heat and add the chickpeas, lime juice, and cilantro. Taste and add salt, if desired.

4. Serve over rice, your favorite whole grain, or simply on its own.

ASPARAGUS, GOAT CHEESE, AND CHIVE QUICHE

PREP TIME: 3 hours 30 minutes (mostly inactive) | COOK TIME: 1 hour 30 minutes
TOTAL TIME: 5 hours (mostly inactive) | YIELD: 8 to 10 servings

Asparagus, goat cheese, and chives are a trio made in quiche heaven. I've used a delicate and flaky pâte brisée tart dough as the base, though you can use a premade crust (if so, skip directly to step four). Also, please note that this is not a deep-dish-pie recipe. Use a 9 x 1-inch fluted tart or pie dish.

FOR THE TART DOUGH:

5 ounces (1 cup) all-purpose flour, plus more for dusting

3 ounces (6 tablespoons) unsalted butter, cubed and cold

½ teaspoon kosher salt

3 tablespoons cold water

FOR THE FILLING:

10 medium or 13 thin asparagus stalks (3 to 4 ounces), tough ends removed

1 tablespoon chopped fresh chives (scallions may be substituted)

⅓ cup crumbled soft goat cheese

1 cup heavy cream

4 large eggs

½ teaspoon kosher salt

⅛ teaspoon ground black pepper

Pinch of fresh-grated nutmeg

1. Add the flour, butter, and salt to a food processor. Pulse the machine on and off until the mixture is crumbly. With the machine running, slowly add the water until just combined (do not overmix). Wrap the dough in plastic wrap and press flat into a disk. Chill for at least 2 hours, or overnight.

2. Preheat the oven to 400°F. Allow the dough to rest at room temperature for 5 minutes. On a lightly floured surface, roll the dough to approximately ¼ inch. Carefully place in a 9 x 1-inch fluted tart pan or pie dish. Place the tart pan in the refrigerator and chill for 30 minutes.

3. Place the tart pan on a baking sheet. Use a fork to poke holes throughout the bottom of the dough to prevent air bubbles from forming. Line the tart pan with foil, covering the dough, and pour uncooked beans into the center, as if it were filling (weighting down the dough keeps it from bubbling and expanding). Bake for 20 minutes, removing the beans and foil for the last 5 minutes. Remove and allow to cool while preparing the filling.

4. If using a premade crust, follow baking directions on the package and set aside. Preheat the oven to 350°F. Slice the asparagus in half. Leave the top halves intact and cut the bottoms into ¼-inch pieces. Bring a pot of water to a boil and set out a bowl with ice water. Blanch the asparagus

recipe continued on page 202

(both the top halves and bottom pieces) in the boiling water for 1 minute. Drain and then place in an ice bath to halt the cooking process.

5. Spread ½ tablespoon of the chives evenly in the bottom of the baked pie crust. Sprinkle the goat cheese evenly on top, followed by the chopped asparagus, reserving the top halves of the stalks for decoration.

6. In a medium bowl, whisk the cream, eggs, salt, pepper, and nutmeg. Stir in the remaining ½ tablespoon chives. Pour the custard mixture into the tart shell and then gently lay the top halves of the asparagus on top in a decorative manner.

7. Bake the quiche for 45 to 55 minutes, or until no longer liquid but still slightly jiggly in the center. Allow to cool for at least 25 minutes before serving so the custard can fully set.

Cake is the only thing that matters.
—Allie Brosh

SWEETS AND TREATS

I enjoyed sweets when I was younger, but I was a child of the eighties, so my favorites were usually processed candies and novelties. I loved strawberry fruit roll-ups, Pop Rocks, and Pixy Stix. As I grew older, I became less interested in desserts. If you had asked me ten years ago whether I preferred sweet or savory foods, I would have answered savory without hesitation. I named my blog *Savory Simple* and picked the culinary arts program over the pastry program at my school. As time has passed, the answer is no longer simple. I developed a massive sweet tooth at culinary school and a passion for creating desserts that sometimes surpasses my interest in cooking. There is a Zen quality to baking that calms me when I'm anxious. There is a level of satisfaction I feel when tasting a homemade slice of layer cake that I never quite get from my other recipes.

In this chapter you'll see some recurring themes: ice creams, curds, shortbreads, and meringue buttercreams. These are some of my absolute favorite desserts to prepare, share with guests, and enjoy on my own. I also frequently add alcohol, especially sweet liqueurs, to desserts. Alcohol often can be omitted, but consider that if you remove alcohol from baked goods, you will want to increase one of the other liquids (for example, the cream) so the dry-to-liquid ratio remains the same.

I won't sugarcoat this (pun intended): most of my layer cakes are fairly advanced recipes, but try not to be intimidated. Baking is a skill that takes patience, practice, and a willingness to experiment. Once mastered, it is both relaxing and fun. I promise! A beautiful dessert is a work of art that is meant to be shared with friends and family.

VANILLA BEAN BOURBON ICE CREAM

PREP TIME: 8 hours 10 minutes (mostly inactive) | **COOK TIME:** 10 minutes
TOTAL TIME: 8 hours 20 minutes (mostly inactive) | **YIELD:** Approximately 1 quart

Vanilla and bourbon are a seriously delicious flavor combination. You have to be careful when adding alcohol to frozen desserts such as ice cream. Alcohol lowers the freezing point, which can prevent the ice cream from firming up while churning. However, when added in the right quantity it has a different, more desirable effect; it keeps the ice cream soft and prevents it from getting too firm. When alcohol is added to ice cream, you can scoop it immediately after removing it from the freezer, though you might notice it melting a bit faster than normal. In very small quantities, neutral alcohols such as vodka can be added to adjust the texture without changing the flavor. This recipe pushes the limits of how much alcohol can be added so you can really taste the bourbon.

2 cups half-and-half, or 1 cup whole milk plus 1 cup heavy cream

2 teaspoons pure vanilla extract

1 vanilla bean

5 large egg yolks

½ cup granulated sugar

1 tablespoon light brown sugar

¼ cup bourbon

1. Combine the half-and-half and vanilla extract in a medium saucepan.

2. Use a small paring knife to split the vanilla bean in half lengthwise. Use the dull edge of the knife to scrape out the seeds before adding the seeds and vanilla bean pod to the saucepan. Turn the heat to medium.

3. While the liquid is coming to a simmer, place the yolks and both sugars into a medium bowl and whisk vigorously to combine.

4. When the cream has just barely reached a simmer, turn the heat down to low and use tongs to remove the vanilla bean pod. Ladle half of the hot cream into the yolk mixture while whisking to temper the eggs and prevent them from scrambling. To create the ice cream base, pour the ingredients in the bowl back into the saucepan, using a spatula to scrape any remaining yolk and sugar from the sides of the bowl.

recipe continued on page 208

5. With the heat still on low, stir the ice cream base continuously until it has thickened slightly, 5 to 7 minutes, and then stir in the bourbon. Remove from the heat and allow to cool for 5 to 10 minutes, stirring periodically. Cover with plastic wrap, pressing the film directly onto the ice cream base to prevent a skin from forming. Chill in the refrigerator until very cold, preferably overnight.

6. Prepare in an ice cream maker according to the manufacturer's instructions. The ice cream will be a soft-serve consistency straight from the machine; continue chilling in the freezer to firm up.

SALTED CARAMEL TOFFEE ICE CREAM

PREP TIME: 8 hours 15 minutes (mostly inactive) | COOK TIME: 15 minutes
TOTAL TIME: 8 hours 30 minutes (mostly inactive) | YIELD: Approximately 1 quart

Proper caramelization takes a bit of practice and, in the beginning, a willingness to be brave. There's a fine line between good caramel, burned caramel, and sugars that haven't been caramelized enough. This refers to both dessert caramels that use sugar and savories such as caramelized onions, where natural sugars are going through the same browning process. If you don't push the caramelization process enough, the sugar remains too sweet. Good caramel is slightly sweet but also very bitter. That bitter/sweet balance is what makes this ice cream so good, especially once the sweet, crunchy toffee bits are added. While bourbon is not an essential ingredient, adding alcohol to frozen desserts lowers the freezing point, making it easier to scoop right out of the freezer.

¾ cup granulated sugar

2 tablespoons water

1 teaspoon kosher salt

1 cup heavy cream, room temperature

1 cup whole milk, room temperature

7 large egg yolks

1 tablespoon bourbon (optional)

8 ounces toffee bits, such as Heath

1. In a medium saucepan, heat ½ cup of the sugar, the water, and salt over medium heat until the sugar has dissolved. Allow the sugar to continue cooking, watching it closely, until it starts to turn golden brown. Once it begins to caramelize, it will continue to darken quickly. You want to let the sugar get as dark as possible without burning for best results. Wait until the caramel is a dark amber color, and then remove the pan from the heat and pour the cream down the side of the saucepan. The caramel will splatter so be very careful to avoid burns. It also will temporarily seize up and solidify when the colder cream is added. Move the pan back onto the burner and use a heatproof spatula to stir the caramel and cream until evenly combined. Stir in the milk and remove from the heat.

2. In a large bowl, whisk the egg yolks with the remaining ¼ cup sugar. Allow the caramel sauce to come to a gentle simmer, and then turn the heat down to low. Add several ladles of the caramel sauce to the yolk mixture while whisking. Pour the mixture back into the saucepan, using a spatula to scrape out any remaining yolk and sugar; this is your ice cream base.

recipe continued on page 211

3. With the heat still on low, stir the ice cream base continuously until it has thickened slightly, 5 to 7 minutes. Remove from the heat, stir in the bourbon if using, and allow to cool for 5 to 10 minutes, stirring periodically. Pour the liquid into a clean bowl and cover with plastic wrap, pressing the film directly onto the ice cream surface to prevent a skin from forming. Chill in the refrigerator until very cold, preferably overnight.

4. Prepare in an ice cream maker according to the manufacturer's instructions. When the ice cream is almost finished churning, add the toffee bits. The ice cream will be a soft-serve consistency straight from the machine; continue chilling in the freezer to firm up.

ROASTED BLUEBERRY
CRÈME FRAÎCHE ICE CREAM

PREP TIME: 8 hours 10 minutes (mostly inactive) | **COOK TIME:** 25 minutes | **TOTAL TIME:** 8 hours 35 minutes (mostly inactive) | **YIELD:** Approximately 1 quart

I frequently use crème fraîche in both sweet and savory recipes. It often can be found in the cheese aisle at grocery stores. Crème fraîche is very similar to sour cream but the flavor is more delicate and subtle. It gives this ice cream an incredibly rich texture and very slight sour note that offsets the sweetness of the roasted blueberries. The bright color of the ice cream combined with its bold flavor make it a major crowd pleaser.

18 ounces (approximately 3 cups) fresh blueberries

6 large egg yolks

¾ cup granulated sugar

1¼ cups whole milk

½ teaspoon pure vanilla extract

8 ounces crème fraîche (full-fat sour cream may be substituted)

1. Preheat the oven to 400°F. Line a baking sheet with aluminum foil.

2. Place the blueberries on the baking sheet. Roast for 12 minutes, shaking the pan every 4 minutes for even cooking. Remove from the oven and allow to cool. Puree the blueberries in a blender until smooth and set aside.

3. In a large bowl, whisk the egg yolks and sugar.

4. Add the milk and vanilla to a saucepan on medium heat. When the mixture is just starting to simmer (do not let it come to a boil), turn the heat to low. Slowly ladle the liquid into the yolks while whisking.

5. Pour the mixture back into the saucepan and stir with a heatproof rubber spatula for 3 to 5 minutes until slightly thickened. Remove from the heat and whisk in the crème fraîche until smooth. Stir in the blueberry puree. Allow to cool for 5 to 10 minutes, stirring periodically. Cover with plastic wrap pressed directly against the liquid to prevent a skin from forming. Chill until very cold, preferably overnight.

6. Prepare in an ice cream maker according to the manufacturer's instructions. The ice cream will be a soft-serve consistency out of the machine; continue chilling in the freezer to firm up.

MALTED CONDENSED MILK ICE CREAM

PREP TIME: 8 hours 30 minutes (mostly inactive) | COOK TIME: 10 minutes
TOTAL TIME: 8 hours 40 minutes (mostly inactive) | YIELD: Approximately 1 quart

I get excited about malt desserts, and I especially enjoy the flavor in this ice cream. This recipe packs a powerful punch; I've more than doubled the amount of malt from when it first appeared on my blog. After making it several times, I decided that while this ice cream is a bit unusual, it's one of my favorites. The sweetened condensed milk and malt combine for an almost sticky, viscous texture. It's very sweet, but not cloyingly so. The sweetened condensed milk also helps keep the ice cream at a lower freezing point so it's easy to scoop right out of the freezer.

6 large egg yolks

1 (14-ounce) can sweetened condensed milk

2½ cups half-and-half, or 1¼ cups whole milk plus 1¼ cups heavy cream

1½ teaspoons pure vanilla extract

⅔ cup malted milk powder

1. In a large bowl, whisk the egg yolks and condensed milk until smooth.

2. In a medium saucepan, heat the half-and-half and vanilla until it just begins to simmer, then turn the heat to low. Ladle approximately half of the half-and-half mixture into the egg yolks while whisking. Pour the mixture back into the saucepan, using a spatula to scrape out the bowl.

3. Slowly whisk in the malted milk powder until evenly combined. Switch to a heatproof spatula and stir over low heat for several minutes, until the mixture begins to slightly thicken.

4. Remove from the heat, pour the liquid into a bowl, and allow it to cool for several minutes, stirring occasionally. Place plastic wrap directly against the top of the liquid to prevent a skin from forming. Chill in the refrigerator until very cold, preferably overnight.

5. Prepare in an ice cream maker according to the manufacturer's instructions. The ice cream will be a soft-serve consistency straight from the machine; continue chilling in the freezer to firm up.

ESPRESSO GRANITA WITH WHIPPED SWEETENED CONDENSED MILK

PREP TIME: 3 to 4 hours (mostly inactive) | **TOTAL TIME:** 3 to 4 hours (mostly inactive)
YIELD: 5 to 6 servings

A granita is an Italian ice dessert made from sugar, water, and various flavorings. Occasionally you'll see savory or tart versions served at restaurants as "palette cleansers," but more often than not, granitas are sweet. Years ago, a friend introduced me to a Vietnamese coffee drink called *café su da* or *cà-phê sũa dá*. It's iced dark-roasted Vietnamese coffee (or sometimes chicory coffee) served with a healthy amount of sweetened condensed milk. This dessert is inspired by that drink. I've used espresso, but you can substitute a dark-roasted coffee if you prefer. Decaffeinated espressos and coffees always taste off to me, so I prefer sticking with regular versions unless you'll be serving this granita late in the evening.

3 cups freshly brewed espresso

¼ cup granulated sugar

Pinch of kosher salt

1½ cups heavy whipping cream, cold

¼ cup sweetened condensed milk

Bittersweet chocolate for garnish

1. In a large bowl, whisk the espresso, sugar, and salt. More sugar may be added, but remember that the condensed milk topping will be very sweet.

2. Pour the liquid into an 8 x 8 brownie pan or flat-bottomed dish. Place in the freezer for 30 minutes. Stir the mixture very thoroughly with a fork and allow it to freeze for another 30 minutes. Repeat this process every 30 minutes for a total of 3 to 4 hours, making sure to scrape down the sides of the pan.

3. Place the cream in a stand mixer fitted with a whisk attachment and whip to a stiff peak. Alternately, the cream can be whipped by hand using a large bowl and a whisk. Use a spatula to slowly fold in the condensed milk until evenly combined.

4. Divide the espresso granita evenly among serving cups. Top with the whipped cream. Grate some bittersweet chocolate on top and serve.

BUTTERMILK PANNA COTTA WITH RASPBERRY COULIS

PREP TIME: 3 hours 20 minutes (mostly inactive) | **COOK TIME:** 5 minutes | **TOTAL TIME:** 3 hours 25 minutes (mostly inactive) | **YIELD:** 6 servings

This is an excellent dessert to serve dinner guests or present at the end of a romantic home-cooked meal. It looks absolutely beautiful. It's also deceptively easy to make for something with such a fancy name. But perhaps more important, you can prepare the entire recipe in advance, even a day or two beforehand, and have it chilled and ready to serve for dessert. The buttermilk panna cotta is tangy, comforting, and smooth; the coulis is tart and sweet. Any leftover coulis can be stored in the refrigerator for up to five days or in the freezer for several months.

FOR THE PANNA COTTA:

1½ teaspoons unflavored gelatin

1 cup heavy cream or half-and-half

⅓ cup granulated sugar

1 teaspoon pure vanilla extract

2 cups buttermilk

FOR THE COULIS:

¼ cup water

1 teaspoon fresh-squeezed lemon juice

2½ tablespoons granulated sugar

12 ounces frozen raspberries, thawed for 30 minutes

1. To prepare the panna cotta, place the gelatin in a large bowl with 1 tablespoon of lukewarm water to soften for 5 minutes.

2. In a medium saucepan, bring the cream, sugar, and vanilla to a simmer over medium-high heat, stirring until the sugar has dissolved. Remove from the heat and pour into the bowl with the gelatin, whisking to combine. Whisk in the buttermilk.

3. Pour the mixture into 6 wineglasses (or decorative serving glasses of your choice). Carefully place in the refrigerator and chill for a minimum of 3 hours, or overnight.

4. To prepare the coulis, in a small saucepan, bring the water, lemon juice, and sugar to a simmer over medium-high heat, stirring, until the sugar has just dissolved. Remove the syrup from the heat.

5. Place the raspberries in a food processor or high-powered blender along with the sugar syrup and puree until smooth.

6. Press the mixture through a fine mesh strainer or food mill. Discard the raspberry seeds and place the sauce in the refrigerator until the panna cotta is ready to serve.

7. Drizzle the coulis on top of the panna cotta before serving.

BLOOD ORANGE CURD/ORANGE CURD

PREP TIME: 20 minutes | **COOK TIME:** 20 minutes | **TOTAL TIME:** 40 minutes
YIELD: Approximately 2½ cups

I absolutely love homemade curds. Store-bought curds don't compare to homemade versions, which aren't difficult to make. I use curds in a variety of desserts such as cupcakes, cookies, and ice creams. I also serve them on top of biscuits and scones. You might even find me eating homemade curd directly from the bowl with a spoon, it's that good. I use variations of this particular recipe twice in the book: as a filling for Pumpkin-Spiced Cupcakes (page 234) and for Blood Orange Curd Linzer Cookies (page 258). Blood oranges are seasonal and have a slightly different flavor; they're a bit sweeter and less acidic. If you can't find blood oranges or bottled, fresh-squeezed blood orange juice, regular orange juice will always work well as a substitute.

2 large eggs

3 large egg yolks

1 cup granulated sugar

3 tablespoons cornstarch

1 cup fresh-squeezed blood orange (or regular orange) juice

1 to 2 drops red or orange food coloring (optional)

1 tablespoon fresh-squeezed lemon juice (approximately ½ lemon)

4 ounces (8 tablespoons) unsalted butter, cubed and at room temperature

1. In a medium saucepan (preferably heavy bottomed), whisk the eggs, egg yolks, and sugar until smooth. In a separate bowl, whisk the cornstarch with approximately ¼ cup of the orange juice to create a slurry. Whisk the remaining juice and the slurry into the egg mixture along with the lemon juice and food coloring, if using.

2. Turn the heat to medium and continue whisking until thick, 10 to 15 minutes. Make sure the whisk scrapes the bottom of the pan to prevent burning.

3. Remove from the heat and slowly whisk in the butter.

4. Transfer the curd to a clean bowl and press plastic wrap against the top to prevent a skin from forming. Chill in the refrigerator for at least 15 to 20 minutes. The curd will continue to thicken as it cools.

CONCORD GRAPE CURD

PREP TIME: 30 minutes | **COOK TIME:** 35 minutes | **TOTAL TIME:** 1 hour 5 minutes
YIELD: Approximately 2½ cups

Whenever I see Concord grapes, I buy as many as I can because of their brief seasonal availability on the East Coast. To make them last as long as possible, I juice them. Concords have tiny seeds, so the easiest way to remove them is to toss the grapes into a pot, cook them down with some water, and strain out the seeds. I've made a very concentrated juice for this recipe to maximize the flavor of the curd. To drink any leftover juice, I recommend diluting it with water to taste and then adding some sugar if you need additional sweetness (I think they're sweet enough as is, but that's a matter of personal preference).

1 pound Concord grapes

¼ cup water

2 large eggs

4 large egg yolks

1 cup granulated sugar

3 tablespoons cornstarch

1½ teaspoons fresh-squeezed lemon juice (approximately ½ lemon)

4 ounces (8 tablespoons) unsalted butter, cubed and at room temperature

1. Place the grapes and water in a medium saucepan (preferably heavy bottomed) over medium-low heat. Allow the grapes to heat for approximately 10 minutes, stirring periodically. As the grapes begin to break down, use a potato masher to gently press the grapes and release the juices. Once there is a good amount of liquid in the pan, remove from the heat and cool briefly. Press the grapes through a food mill or a fine mesh strainer positioned over a bowl, pressing gently with a spoon or ladle to release the juice. Discard the seeds, skin, and pulp. Reserve 1¼ cups of juice for preparing the curd.

2. In a medium saucepan, whisk the eggs, egg yolks, and sugar until smooth. In a separate bowl, whisk the cornstarch with approximately ¼ cup of the grape juice to create a slurry. Whisk the remaining 1 cup juice, the slurry, and the lemon juice into the egg mixture.

3. Continue whisking over medium heat until thick, 10 to 15 minutes. Make sure the whisk scrapes the bottom of the pan to prevent burning.

4. Remove from the heat and slowly whisk in the butter.

5. Transfer the curd to a bowl, press plastic wrap against the top to prevent a skin from forming, and chill in the refrigerator for at least 15 to 20 minutes. The curd will continue to thicken as it cools.

CHOCOLATE ESPRESSO LAYER CAKE

PREP TIME: 1 hour 30 minutes | **COOK TIME:** 30 minutes | **TOTAL TIME:** 2 hours | **YIELD:** 12 to 16 servings

This is by far my favorite and most requested cake. Chocolate and espresso are complementary flavors, in part because the sweetness offsets the bitterness for a flavor balance that you don't often find in desserts. While any brand of unsweetened cocoa powder will work in this recipe, I recommend using Valrhona if you want the dark brown color shown in these images. It also offers a much deeper chocolate flavor than you will find in grocery store brands. Valrhona cocoa powder can be purchased at many online retailers and gourmet shops. I also like to use a bit of Van Gogh double espresso vodka in both the cake and the buttercream, but regular espresso may be substituted in its place. I strongly recommend weighing the flour with a kitchen scale for consistent results. I also use a revolving cake stand and cardboard cake rounds. While not essential, these make working with the layers and decorating the cake a breeze.

FOR THE CAKE:

10½ ounces (2 cups plus 1½ tablespoons) all-purpose flour

2 tablespoons espresso powder

2 teaspoons baking powder

1½ teaspoons kosher salt

3 ounces (9 tablespoons) unsweetened cocoa powder

1½ cups half-and-half, or ¾ cup cream plus ¾ cup whole milk

¼ cup espresso vodka (room temperature espresso may be substituted)

1½ tablespoons pure vanilla extract

9 ounces (18 tablespoons) unsalted butter, room temperature

2¼ cups granulated sugar

6 large eggs, room temperature

Fresh-grated unsweetened or semisweet chocolate for garnish (optional)

FOR THE BUTTERCREAM:

1½ cups granulated sugar

¼ cup plus 2 tablespoons water

5 large egg whites

1 pound (2 cups) unsalted butter, cubed and at room temperature

3 ounces unsweetened chocolate, melted

1 tablespoon espresso, room temperature

1 tablespoon espresso vodka (regular espresso may be substituted)

recipe continued on next page

PREPARE THE CAKE:

1. Preheat the oven to 350°F. Place an oven rack in the middle position. Lightly spray the bottom of three 8-inch cake pans with baking spray, and cover with parchment rounds. Set aside.

2. In a medium bowl, whisk the flour, espresso powder, baking powder, and salt. Sift in the cocoa powder and whisk until the dry ingredients are evenly combined. In a separate small bowl, combine the half-and-half, espresso vodka, and vanilla.

3. In a stand mixer with the paddle attachment, cream the butter and sugar on low speed for 5 minutes. Add the eggs, one at a time, allowing each egg to fully incorporate before adding the next. Scrape down the sides of the bowl. With the mixer still on low speed, swiftly alternate between adding the dry and liquid ingredients for a minute. Scrape down the sides well, making sure to reach the bottom of the bowl. Turn the mixer on medium speed for 30 seconds.

4. Distribute the batter evenly among the three cake pans, using a spatula to even out the tops.

5. Bake until a toothpick inserted into the center of each cake comes out clean, 30 to 35 minutes. Allow the cakes to cool completely in the pans before removing.

PREPARE THE BUTTERCREAM:

1. Add the sugar and water to a medium pot. Cover and turn the heat to high. Once the liquid begins to simmer and steam has developed, remove the cover (this helps prevent crystallization). Using a candy thermometer, cook the sugar for approximately 5 minutes, until it has reached the soft-ball stage, approximately 235° to 240°F, to form the syrup.

2. While the syrup is cooking, beat the egg whites on high speed in a stand mixer with the whisk attachment, until a soft peak has formed.

3. Turn the mixer speed down to medium-low and very slowly pour the syrup down the side of the bowl into the egg whites. Don't pour the hot syrup directly into the meringue, or the egg whites may scramble.

4. Once the syrup is completely mixed, turn the speed to high and allow the meringue to continue to form a stiff peak while cooling, 15 to 20 minutes. To speed this process, ice packs may be placed around the bowl.

5. Once the meringue is room temperature, slowly begin adding the butter on medium speed. Once all the butter has been mixed, turn the mixer speed up to high and very slowly add the chocolate, espresso, and vodka until incorporated.

ASSEMBLE THE CAKE:

1. Place a cardboard round on a cake stand and top with the first layer of cake (remove the parchment paper).

2. Place approximately 1 cup of buttercream on the cake and spread evenly with an offset spatula. Add more buttercream as needed to reach the desired thickness. Repeat with the second and third layers (don't forget to remove the parchment each time). Use an offset spatula to apply a thin layer of frosting to the sides and top of the cake. Chill in the refrigerator for 30 minutes to set this first layer of buttercream. Cover the entire cake with a final layer of frosting. Grate some unsweetened chocolate on top of the cake for decoration, if desired.

3. Serve the cake at room temperature.

CARAMEL APPLE POUND CAKE

PREP TIME: 15 minutes | **COOK TIME:** 1 hour 15 minutes | **TOTAL TIME:** 1 hour 30 minutes
YIELD: 10 to 12 servings

Apple picking is one of my favorite autumn activities. Even though apples are often available all year at the store, seasonal apples have so much flavor and are wonderful in baked goods. Tart apples are especially good to use because they offer both sweetness and acidity. While I prefer to eat sweet apples, I use tart apples in almost all of my recipes. This caramel apple pound cake is sweet, eggy, and dense, but also quite soft. It has apples in every slice. And it's covered in a rich, creamy caramel sauce that keeps the cake moist and flavorful.

FOR THE CAKE:

6 ounces (1½ cups) cake flour

½ teaspoon kosher salt

½ teaspoon ground cinnamon

8 ounces (16 tablespoons) unsalted butter, room temperature

1⅓ cups granulated sugar

3 large eggs

3 large egg yolks

1 teaspoon pure vanilla extract

2 teaspoons brandy

1 large tart apple, such as Granny Smith

FOR THE CARAMEL SAUCE:

1 cup granulated sugar

¼ cup water

¼ teaspoon kosher salt

¾ cup heavy cream or half-and-half

1. Preheat the oven to 325°F and place an oven rack in the center position. Grease a 9 x 5-inch loaf pan with baking spray or butter and line the bottom with parchment paper.

2. In a small bowl, whisk the flour, salt, and cinnamon. Set aside.

3. In a stand mixer with the paddle attachment, cream the butter and sugar on high speed until light and fluffy, approximately 5 minutes. Scrape down the sides of the bowl and mix on high speed for another 30 seconds. Turn the speed down to medium-low. Add the eggs and yolks, one at a time, allowing each to incorporate completely before adding the next. Scrape down the sides of the bowl all the way to the bottom, add the vanilla and brandy, and mix again until everything is just combined.

4. On low speed, add the dry ingredients in three batches, and mix until the batter is just combined.

5. Peel and core the apple, then slice it in half from top to bottom. With the flat sides down, slice each half thinly.

6. Spread a small amount of the batter into the reserved loaf pan. Layer the apple in the pan, overlapping each other, until the bottom of the pan is covered. Pour in

recipe continued on page 230

the rest of the batter, smoothing the top with a spatula. Place the loaf pan on a baking sheet.

7. Bake for 70 to 75 minutes, or until a toothpick inserted into the center of the cake comes out clean. Allow the cake to cool for 5 minutes in the pan and then gently flip onto a cooling rack. Allow the cake to cool to room temperature.

8. While the cake is cooling, prepare the caramel sauce. In a medium saucepan, heat the sugar, water, and salt over medium heat until the sugar is dissolved. Continue cooking until it starts to turn golden brown. Once it begins to caramelize, it will continue to darken quickly. Let the sugar get as dark as possible without burning for best results.

9. When the caramel is dark amber in color, remove the pan from the heat and pour the cream down the side of the saucepan. The caramel will splatter, so be very careful to avoid burns. The caramel will temporarily seize up and solidify when the cream is added.

10. Move the pan back to the burner and use a heatproof spatula to stir the caramel and cream until evenly combined. Allow the sauce to reduce while stirring, until it reaches the desired thickness, 5 to 10 minutes.

11. Before serving, drizzle the caramel sauce over the cake.

MINI PEACH AMARETTO CREAM CAKES

PREP TIME: 20 minutes | **COOK TIME:** 25 minutes | **TOTAL TIME:** 45 minutes | **YIELD:** 12 cakes

I realize that people might look at this recipe for mini cakes and think "she means cupcakes, right?" It's true; these are not overwhelmingly different from cupcakes. But I've tried to create something that feels a bit more like a single-serving layer cake. And, full disclosure, I saw Donna Hay do this in one of her cookbooks and I am stealing the concept because I love it. The amaretto can be omitted if you can't use alcohol, but it's a great complement to the peaches and adds a very unique flavor to the dessert. As far as whether to peel the peaches, I almost never peel them—I like peach skins. However, you can quickly peel them by cutting a small X at the base, and then blanching them in boiling water for 15 to 20 seconds, until the skin loosens. After that, use a slotted spoon to move the peaches to an ice bath and peel them by hand.

FOR THE CAKES:

8 ounces (1½ cups) all-purpose flour

1 teaspoon baking powder

¼ teaspoon kosher salt

6 ounces (12 tablespoons) unsalted butter, room temperature

⅔ cup granulated sugar

1 teaspoon pure vanilla extract

3 large eggs

1 ripe peach, finely chopped (peeled or unpeeled, depending on preference), plus 1 thinly sliced ripe peach for garnish

FOR THE AMARETTO CREAM:

1 cup heavy cream

1½ tablespoons amaretto

½ teaspoon pure vanilla extract

1½ teaspoons granulated sugar

1. Preheat the oven to 325°F and place an oven rack in the middle position. Grease a large muffin tin with baking spray or butter and place on a baking sheet.

2. In a medium bowl, whisk the flour, baking soda, and salt.

3. In a stand mixer fitted with the paddle attachment, cream the butter and sugar on high speed until light and fluffy, approximately 5 minutes. Turn the speed down to low and add the vanilla, followed by the eggs, one at a time, allowing each egg to fully incorporate before adding the next. Scrape down the sides of the bowl, all the way to the bottom. The batter may look slightly broken. Turn the mixer to medium and add the dry ingredients in three batches, until just combined. Scrape down the bowl again to ensure no flour remains.

4. Distribute the batter evenly into the muffin tin and bake for 20 to 25 minutes, or until a toothpick inserted into the center of a cake comes out clean. Allow to cool for 5 minutes in the muffin tin before removing the cakes and placing on a wire rack to finish cooling.

recipe continued on page 233

5. To prepare the amaretto cream, in a large bowl, beat the heavy cream with a whisk until it reaches a soft peak. Add the amaretto, vanilla, and sugar and briefly whisk again to combine.

6. Once the cakes have reached room temperature, slice in half lengthwise. Spread half the amaretto cream onto the centers of each cake and top evenly with the chopped peaches. Place the tops of the cakes over the peaches and spread the remaining amaretto cream on top. Garnish with the sliced peaches.

PUMPKIN-SPICED CUPCAKES
WITH ORANGE CURD

PREP TIME: 55 minutes | **COOK TIME:** 40 minutes | **TOTAL TIME:** 1 hour 35 minutes | **YIELD:** 24 cupcakes

Have you ever tried a curd-filled cupcake? It's pretty awesome. If you're not as smitten with homemade curd as I am, you can omit the filling from this recipe to simplify things. But I really recommend it. I've opted for a basic frosting instead of my normal Italian meringue buttercream since the recipe has three components. You don't have to make everything at once; the curd and cupcakes can be made up to seventy-two hours in advance. For best results, I recommend preparing the buttercream frosting on the same day you plan on piping the cupcakes. This recipe is perfect for fall and winter celebrations.

FOR THE CUPCAKES:

7 ounces (1¼ cup plus 2 tablespoons) all-purpose flour

1 ounce (6 tablespoons) cornstarch

1½ teaspoons baking powder

1 teaspoon kosher salt

2 tablespoons pumpkin pie spice

Grated zest from 1 orange (reserve 1 teaspoon for buttercream)

1 cup half-and-half, or ½ cup whole milk plus ½ cup heavy cream

1 tablespoon pure vanilla extract

¼ cup pumpkin puree

6 ounces (12 tablespoons) unsalted butter, room temperature

1¾ cups granulated sugar

4 large eggs

Approximately 1 cup homemade orange curd (page 221)

FOR THE BUTTERCREAM:

10 ounces (20 tablespoons) unsalted butter, room temperature

2½ cups confectioners' sugar

½ teaspoon pure vanilla extract

¼ cup fresh-squeezed orange juice

1 teaspoon grated orange zest

2 teaspoons pumpkin pie spice

Pinch of kosher salt

1. Line two large muffin tins with cupcake liners (optional: to ensure the cupcakes don't stick to the liners, lightly coat the insides with baking spray). Preheat the oven to 350°F and place the oven racks in the upper-middle and lower-middle positions.

2. In a medium bowl, whisk the flour, cornstarch, baking powder, salt, pumpkin pie spice, and orange zest (use your fingers to break apart any clumps of zest).

recipe continued on page 236

3. In a small bowl, combine the half-and-half, vanilla, and pumpkin puree.

4. In a stand mixer fitted with the paddle attachment, cream the butter and sugar on high speed until light and fluffy, 3 to 5 minutes. Turn the speed to low and add the eggs, one at a time, while periodically scraping down the sides of the bowl. Allow each egg to incorporate completely before adding the next.

5. On medium-low speed, alternate between adding the dry and wet ingredients for approximately 60 seconds. Scrape down the bowl one more time, all the way to the bottom, to make sure no patches of flour remain.

6. Evenly distribute the batter among the cupcake liners. Bake for 21 to 23 minutes, or until a toothpick inserted into the center of one of the cupcakes comes out clean.

7. Allow the cupcakes to cool completely and then remove from the pan. Use a paring knife to core each cupcake. Before frosting the cupcakes, use a pastry bag (or a plastic bag with the corner snipped off) to fill each cupcake with curd.

8. In a stand mixer fitted with a paddle attachment, mix the butter at medium-high speed for 30 seconds.

9. Add the confectioners' sugar and mix on medium-low speed for approximately 45 seconds. Scrape down the sides and then mix on medium speed until the ingredients are completely combined.

10. Scrape down the bowl and add the vanilla, orange juice, orange zest, pumpkin pie spice, and salt. Mix on medium speed to incorporate the ingredients and then turn the mixer to medium-high speed and mix for 4 to 5 minutes, or until light and fluffy. Scrape down the sides of the bowl once or twice during this process.

11. Place the buttercream in a pastry bag with a decorative tip of your choice. Pipe the buttercream evenly onto each cupcake and serve.

PINEAPPLE CAKE

PREP TIME: 15 minutes | **COOK TIME:** 1 hour | **TOTAL TIME:** 1 hour 15 minutes
YIELD: 10 to 12 servings

This pineapple cake is fast, easy, and wonderful. It tastes eggy like a pound cake but with a softer texture similar to butter cake. Don't let the little cracks on top fool you; the cake is incredibly moist. It has an entire twenty-ounce can of crushed pineapple mixed into the batter, including the juice. And yes, I know that sounds like a lot. It is. But trust me, the cake holds together. You're looking at it. If you have sliced pineapple or pineapple chunks (the canned variety), you can make crushed pineapple by pulsing it in a food processor until it's broken down. Make sure to use pineapple canned in juice, not syrup. I don't think this cake needs any frosting, but if you'd like to serve it with a condiment, I recommend some freshly whipped, barely sweetened cream.

10 ounces (2 cups) all-purpose flour

2 tablespoons cornstarch

1 teaspoon baking powder

¼ teaspoon kosher salt

Grated zest of 1 lemon

7 ounces (14 tablespoons) unsalted butter, room temperature

¾ cup granulated sugar

4 large eggs

1 (20-ounce) can crushed pineapple in juice (do not drain)

1 teaspoon pure vanilla extract

Freshly whipped cream for serving (optional)

1. Preheat the oven to 350°F and place an oven rack in the middle position. Grease a 9-inch round cake pan with baking spray or butter and line it with parchment paper. Place the cake pan on a baking sheet.

2. In a medium bowl, whisk the flour, cornstarch, baking powder, salt, and lemon zest (use your fingers to break apart any clumps of zest). Set aside.

3. In a stand mixer fitted with the paddle attachment, cream the butter and sugar for several minutes, until light and fluffy; begin on low speed and gradually increase the speed to medium-high. Turn off the mixer and scrape down the sides of the bowl with a spatula.

4. Turn the mixer back to low speed and add the eggs, one at a time, scraping down the bowl after adding the second egg. Allow the eggs to incorporate completely and then scrape down the bowl again. The batter may look slightly broken.

5. Add the crushed pineapple along with the vanilla and mix briefly on medium-low to combine. With the mixer on low, add the flour mixture in three batches, and mix until just

recipe continued on page 239

combined. Turn off the stand mixer and scrape down the bowl with a spatula, giving the batter one final stir.

6. Pour the batter into the cake pan and use a spatula to level off the top.

7. Bake for 50 to 60 minutes, or until a toothpick inserted into the center of the cake comes out clean. Allow to cool for at least 15 minutes before removing the cake from the pan. Serve on its own or topped with whipped cream, if desired.

STRAWBERRY GRAND MARNIER
MINI LAYER CAKE

PREP TIME: 1 hour 30 minutes | **COOK TIME:** 30 minutes | **TOTAL TIME:** 2 hours | **YIELD:** 4 servings

The first time I saw a mini layer cake, I knew it was something I wanted to re-create at home. Luckily, tiny cake pans are readily available and inexpensive. While layer cakes are one of my favorite desserts, I usually find myself giving away most of the leftovers because one can only eat so much cake (sadly). These days, I often bake mini layer cakes because I get to enjoy the beauty of the finished product while keeping the portions reasonable. This triple-layer cake is a wonderful dessert for Valentine's Day, a romantic meal, or an intimate dinner party. I strongly recommend weighing the flour with a kitchen scale for consistent results.

FOR THE CAKE:

4½ ounces (1 scant cup) all-purpose flour

½ teaspoon baking powder

¼ teaspoon kosher salt

½ cup half-and-half, or ¼ cup heavy cream plus ¼ cup whole milk

1½ tablespoons Grand Marnier liqueur

1 teaspoon pure vanilla extract

3 ounces (6 tablespoons) unsalted butter, room temperature

1 scant cup granulated sugar

2 large eggs

⅓ cup finely diced strawberries

FOR THE FILLING/TOPPING:

½ cup finely diced strawberries

½ cup thinly sliced strawberries

1 tablespoon Grand Marnier liqueur

FOR THE BUTTERCREAM:

½ cup granulated sugar

2 tablespoons water

3 large egg whites

8 ounces (16 tablespoons) unsalted butter, cubed and at room temperature

⅓ to ½ cup pureed strawberries (8 to 10 fresh or frozen strawberries)

2 to 3 tablespoons Grand Marnier liqueur

2 to 3 drops red food coloring (optional)

PREPARE THE CAKE:

1. Preheat the oven to 350°F. Place an oven rack in the middle position. Grease the bottoms of three 4 x 2-inch cake pans with baking spray or butter and then cover with parchment rounds. Place on a baking sheet and set aside.

recipe continued on page 242

2. In a medium bowl, whisk the flour, baking powder, and salt. In a separate small bowl, combine the half-and-half, Grand Marnier, and vanilla.

3. In a stand mixer fitted with the paddle attachment, cream the butter and sugar on low speed for 5 minutes. Add the eggs, one at a time, allowing each egg to incorporate before adding the next. Scrape down the sides of the bowl. With the mixer still on low speed, swiftly alternate between adding the dry and liquid ingredients for 1 minute. Scrape down the sides well, making sure to reach the bottom of the bowl. Turn the mixer on medium speed for 30 seconds. Stir in the ⅓ cup finely diced strawberries by hand until combined.

4. Distribute the batter evenly among the three cake pans, using a spatula to even out the tops.

5. Bake until a toothpick inserted into the center of each cake comes out clean, 27 to 30 minutes. Allow the cakes to cool completely in the pan before removing.

PREPARE THE FILLING:

1. Place the finely diced strawberries and thinly sliced strawberries in two separate bowls. Add 1½ teaspoons of the Grand Marnier liqueur to each bowl and stir to combine.

2. Cover each bowl and place in the refrigerator. Allow the berries to soak in the liqueur for at least 30 minutes (see note).

PREPARE THE BUTTERCREAM:

1. Add the sugar and water to a medium saucepan. Cover and turn the heat to high. Once the liquid begins to simmer and steam has developed, remove the cover (this helps prevent crystallization). Using a candy thermometer, cook the sugar to the soft-ball stage, 235° to 240°F, approximately 5 minutes.

2. While the sugar is cooking, whisk the egg whites on high in a stand mixer with the whisk attachment until a soft peak has formed.

3. Turn the mixer speed down to medium-low and very slowly pour the syrup down the side of the bowl into the egg whites. Do not pour the hot syrup directly into the meringue, as the egg whites may scramble.

4. Once the syrup is completely incorporated, turn the speed to high and allow the meringue to continue to form a stiff peak while cooling down to room temperature, 15 to 20 minutes. To speed up this process, ice packs may be placed around the bowl.

5. Once the meringue is at room temperature, slowly add the butter on medium speed. When all of the butter has been incorporated, turn the mixer speed to high and very slowly add the strawberry puree, Grand Marnier, and food coloring, if using.

ASSEMBLE THE CAKE:

1. Place the first layer of cake on a revolving cake stand on top of a cardboard round and remove the parchment paper.

2. Spread approximately ¼ cup of buttercream on the cake and spread it around evenly with an offset spatula. Add more buttercream as needed to reach the desired thickness. Add ¼ cup of the diced strawberries, spreading around evenly without disturbing the frosting. Repeat with the second and third layer (don't forget to remove the parchment each time). Use an offset spatula to apply a very thin layer of frosting to the side and top of the cake. Chill the cake in the refrigerator for 30 minutes to set this first layer of buttercream.

3. Cover the entire cake with a final layer of frosting. Just before serving, top the cake with the sliced strawberries.

4. Cake is best when served at room temperature.

Notes: The cakes can be prepared up to 48 hours in advance.

The berries can be prepared up to 48 hours in advance.

BANANA PEANUT BUTTER LAYER CAKE WITH CHOCOLATE GANACHE

PREP TIME: 1 hour 30 minutes | **COOK TIME:** 40 minutes | **TOTAL TIME:** 2 hours 10 minutes
YIELD: 12 to 16 servings

I always recommend serving cakes at room temperature, especially when they're topped with buttercream. That rule is especially important with this triple-layer cake because you want the ganache topping to be soft when a knife slices through it. Otherwise it will crack into pieces. The ganache is not only beautiful and impressive, it's much easier than the fancy piping seen on many decorative cakes. And it doesn't need to be perfect (in fact, I think it looks better when the drips are scattered and uneven). I recommend using regular peanut butter for this recipe as opposed to one of the "natural" brands that separate and need to be stirred before using. Buttercream can be a fickle thing, and a stable peanut butter will result in a very stable buttercream. I strongly recommend weighing the flour with a kitchen scale for consistent results.

FOR THE CAKE:

12½ ounces (2½ cups) all-purpose flour

2 teaspoons baking powder

1 teaspoon kosher salt

1½ cups mashed ripe bananas (3 to 4 medium)

1½ teaspoons pure vanilla extract

1½ teaspoons spiced rum, such as Captain Morgan Spiced Rum (or substitute additional vanilla extract)

8 ounces (16 tablespoons) unsalted butter, room temperature

2 cups granulated sugar

4 large eggs, room temperature

FOR THE BUTTERCREAM:

1 cup granulated sugar

¼ cup water

4 large egg whites

13 ounces (26 tablespoons) unsalted butter, room temperature

1 teaspoon pure vanilla extract

½ to 1 cup creamy peanut butter

FOR THE GANACHE:

4 ounces bittersweet chocolate, coarsely chopped

2½ ounces (5 tablespoons) unsalted butter, room temperature, cut into small cubes

PREPARE THE CAKE:

1. Preheat the oven to 350°F and place an oven rack in the middle position. Lightly grease the bottoms of three 8-inch cake pans with baking spray or butter and cover with parchment rounds. Set aside.

recipe continued on next page

2. In a medium bowl, whisk the flour, baking powder, and salt. In a separate small bowl, combine the bananas, vanilla, and rum.

3. In a stand mixer fitted with the paddle attachment, cream the butter and sugar on low speed for 5 minutes. Add the eggs, one at a time, allowing each egg to incorporate before adding the next. Scrape down the sides of the bowl. With the mixer still on low speed, swiftly alternate between adding the dry and wet ingredients for a minute. Scrape down the sides, making sure to reach the bottom of the bowl. Turn the mixer up to medium speed for 30 seconds.

4. Distribute the batter evenly among the three cake pans, using a spatula to even out the tops.

5. Bake until a toothpick inserted into the center of each cake comes out clean, 29 to 33 minutes. Allow the cakes to cool completely in the pan before removing.

PREPARE THE BUTTERCREAM:

1. To form the syrup, add the sugar and water to a medium saucepan. Cover and turn the heat to high. Once the liquid begins to simmer and is giving off steam, remove the cover (this helps prevent crystallization). Using a candy thermometer, cook the sugar to the soft-ball stage, 235° to 240°F, approximately 5 minutes.

2. While the sugar is turning to syrup, beat the egg whites on high speed in a stand mixer with the whisk attachment, until a soft peak has formed.

3. Turn the mixer speed down to medium-low and very slowly pour the syrup down the side of the bowl into the egg whites. Don't pour the hot syrup directly into the meringue or the egg whites might scramble.

4. Once the syrup is completely incorporated, turn the speed to high and allow the meringue to continue to form a stiff peak while cooling to room temperature, 15 to 20 minutes. To speed up this process, ice packs may be placed around the bowl.

5. Once the meringue has come to room temperature, slowly begin incorporating the soft butter on medium speed. Once all the butter has been mixed, turn the mixer speed up to high and slowly add the vanilla, followed by the peanut butter, 1 tablespoon at a time. After adding in ½ cup, taste the buttercream for flavor. Add additional peanut butter to taste, 1 tablespoon at a time.

ASSEMBLE THE CAKE:

1. Place a cardboard round on the cake stand and top with the first layer of cake (remove the parchment paper).

2. Spread approximately 1 cup of buttercream evenly on the cake with a spatula. Repeat with the second and third layers (don't forget to remove the parchment each time). Use an offset spatula to apply a thin layer of frosting to the side and top of the cake. Chill in the refrigerator for 30 minutes to set this first layer of buttercream. Cover the entire cake with a final layer of frosting and place in the refrigerator to chill.

PREPARE THE GANACHE:

1. Place the chocolate and butter in a medium heatproof bowl over a pot of simmering water.

2. Using a heatproof spatula, stir the mixture until melted and smooth.

3. Allow the glaze to cool for 2 to 3 minutes. Starting at the center and moving outward in a circular motion, pour the glaze over the chilled cake, smoothing the top with a small offset spatula.

4. Serve the cake at room temperature.

ORANGE BLOSSOM MADELEINES

PREP TIME: 10 minutes | **COOK TIME:** 13 minutes | **TOTAL TIME:** 23 minutes | **YIELD:** 24 madeleines

Orange blossom is such an amazing ingredient to use in desserts. It's a strong flavor, and it's important to note that the potency of the extract will diminish over time. If you have a bottle of orange blossom extract that has been sitting in the refrigerator for more than six months, it will give the cookies a subtler taste than those that are made with fresh extract. Madeleines are technically more like little cakes than like cookies and they are absolutely perfect for dipping in tea.

4½ ounces (1 scant cup) all-purpose flour

1 teaspoon baking powder

½ teaspoon ground coriander

½ cup granulated sugar

3 large eggs, room temperature

1 large egg yolk, room temperature

1½ teaspoons orange blossom extract

1½ tablespoons fresh-squeezed orange juice

4 ounces (8 tablespoons) unsalted butter, melted and cooled

1 teaspoon grated orange zest

⅛ teaspoon kosher salt

Confectioners' sugar for serving

1. Preheat the oven to 350°F. Lightly grease two madeleine pans with baking spray or butter and place on a baking sheet.

2. In a medium bowl, whisk the flour, baking powder, coriander, and sugar. In a large bowl, whisk the eggs, egg yolk, orange blossom extract, and orange juice.

3. Sift the dry ingredients into the wet, whisking until smooth. Whisk in the butter, orange zest, and salt.

4. Fill each well in the madeleine pan with 1 tablespoon batter. Bake for 13 minutes, or until the tops spring back to the touch and are just barely browning around the edges.

5. Allow to cool in the pan for 2 minutes and then turn the cookies out onto a cooling rack.

6. Once cool, dust with confectioners' sugar.

CHERRY VANILLA JAM CRUMB BARS

PREP TIME: 1 hour (mostly inactive) | **COOK TIME:** 25 minutes
TOTAL TIME: 1 hour 25 minutes (mostly inactive) | **YIELD:** 12 bars

Homemade jam takes these shortbread crumb bars to the next level. I've used my recipe for cherry vanilla jam, but any fruit jam will work. Store-bought jams will work in a pinch, but try to find one that comes without processed ingredients (and with as few ingredients over-all). It's also possible to find homemade jams for sale at local markets. These bars are easy to prepare, but a word of caution: make sure that the sides of the pan are very well greased before adding the jam layer. Jam has the potential to bake itself onto the side of the pan, but butter will prevent this from happening.

FOR THE SHORTBREAD BARS:

6 ounces (12 tablespoons) unsalted butter, cubed and at room temperature

2½ ounces (½ cup) confectioners' sugar

½ teaspoon kosher salt

1 teaspoon pure vanilla extract

8½ ounces (1¾ cups) all-purpose flour

1½ cups Cherry Vanilla Bean Jam (page 53)

FOR THE CRUMB TOPPING:

¼ cup all-purpose flour

¼ cup packed light brown sugar

¼ cup toasted slivered almonds, finely chopped

Pinch of kosher salt

2 tablespoons unsalted butter, cold and cut into small pieces

1. Grease an 8 x 8-inch pan with baking spray or butter and line it with parchment paper, allowing the paper to hang over two sides of the pan. Lightly grease the top of the parchment paper as well.

2. Cream the butter, sugar, and salt in a stand mixer on medium-high speed, until light and fluffy. Add the vanilla, turn the mixer to medium-low, and gradually add the flour until the dough is smooth. Briefly stir to ensure the dough is evenly combined.

3. Press the dough evenly into the pan (press the top with plastic wrap to level out). Refrigerate for at least 30 minutes, or overnight.

4. Preheat the oven to 350°F. Bake the shortbread for 25 to 30 minutes, or until lightly golden on top. Allow to cool to room temperature.

5. To prepare the topping, combine the flour, brown sugar, almonds, salt, and butter in a small bowl. Use a fork to mash the ingredients until crumbly.

6. Generously grease the sides of the pan with softened butter to prevent the jam from sticking during the baking process. Spread the cherry vanilla bean jam on top of the shortbread. Evenly distribute the crumb mixture on top.

7. Bake for 20 to 25 minutes, until the topping is brown. Allow to cool completely, before running a knife around the edges of the pan and slicing into 12 bars.

CHOCOLATE BROWNIES
WITH SALTED TAHINI FROSTING

PREP TIME: 20 minutes | **COOK TIME:** 40 minutes | **TOTAL TIME:** 1 hour | **YIELD:** 16 brownies

Tahini is a sesame paste that's more commonly associated with savory recipes such as hummus, but I use it in desserts so often that it appears twice in this book. It adds the same level of richness and nuttiness you'd get from adding peanut butter to a recipe but with a more unique taste. In addition to pairing well with chocolate, it makes a killer buttercream frosting. Tahini can be found in the same aisle as peanut butter in most grocery stores.

FOR THE BROWNIES:

5 ounces bittersweet chocolate, chopped

2½ ounces (5 tablespoons) unsalted butter, cut into small pieces

½ cup granulated sugar

2 large eggs

1½ teaspoons pure vanilla extract

½ teaspoon kosher salt

2 ounces (⅓ cup) all-purpose flour

FOR THE SALTED TAHINI FROSTING:

3 ounces (6 tablespoons) unsalted butter, at room temperature

½ cup well-stirred tahini

¼ cup plus 2 tablespoons confectioners' sugar

¼ teaspoon kosher salt

1. Preheat the oven to 325°F. Grease an 8 x 8-inch brownie pan with baking spray or butter and line it with parchment paper, allowing two sides to hang over the edges.

2. In a large heatproof bowl set over a pot of simmering water, heat the chocolate and butter, stirring until evenly combined and smooth. Remove the pan from the heat.

3. Add the sugar and whisk vigorously until smooth. Whisk in the eggs, vanilla, and salt. Sift in the flour and stir until smooth.

4. Pour the mixture into the pan. Bake for 30 to 35 minutes, or until a toothpick inserted into the center comes out clean. Allow the brownies to cool to room temperature.

5. In a stand mixer fitted with the paddle attachment, cream the butter on high speed until light and fluffy. Add the tahini and mix on medium speed, scraping down the sides several times, until evenly combined with the butter. With the mixer on low speed, add the sugar and salt. Mix until the dry ingredients have incorporated. Scrape down the sides and turn the speed up to medium-high, allowing the frosting to mix for another minute, until light and smooth.

6. Use the excess parchment paper to lift the brownies out of the pan and place them on a cutting board. Use a spatula to evenly frost the brownies. Cut into 16 squares and serve.

LAVENDER VANILLA BEAN PALMIERS

PREP TIME: 30 minutes | **COOK TIME:** 10 minutes | **TOTAL TIME:** 40 minutes | **YIELD:** Approximately 40 cookies

The first time I tried palmiers (also known as elephant ears) was in culinary school. We would make puff pastry from scratch and use it in an assortment of dishes, both sweet and savory. We often used leftover scraps of dough to make these cookies. You can use scraps to prepare this recipe, just note that you might end up with leftover sugar. I buy dried culinary lavender from a local spice shop, but it's easy to find online. Store it in the freezer and it will keep for ages.

1 vanilla bean

1½ cups granulated sugar

1½ teaspoons dried culinary lavender

Pinch of kosher salt

2 sheets puff pastry, chilled

1. Use a small paring knife to slice the vanilla bean in half lengthwise. Use the dull side of the knife to scrape out the seeds.

2. Add the vanilla seeds, sugar, lavender, and salt to a food processor. Pulse several times until the lavender is finely chopped and all the ingredients are combined.

3. Leave the puff pastry in the refrigerator until just before using. Remove one sheet. Sprinkle 2 tablespoons of the lavender sugar on a clean counter and top with the puff pastry. Evenly sprinkle ½ cup of the sugar on top of the puff pastry, and use a rolling pin to gently press the sugar into the dough, thinning the dough out slightly in the process. Gently draw a line down the center of the pastry with a knife or bench scraper to serve as a guide.

4. Starting on one side, tightly roll the dough into the center, constantly pressing the dough to prevent air pockets. Repeat the process on the other side. Wrap parchment paper or plastic wrap around the dough and place in the freezer. Repeat this process with the second puff pastry sheet.

5. Preheat the oven to 450°F. Line a baking sheet with parchment paper.

6. Once the dough is very cold, after it's been in the freezer for 10 to 15 minutes, place one roll on the counter. Carefully slice the dough into thin cookies. Place the cookies on the baking sheet and sprinkle half of the remaining sugar on top. Repeat with the second roll of dough.

7. Bake for 6 minutes or until the bottoms are caramelized. Flip the cookies over and bake for another 3 to 5 minutes.

8. Allow the cookies to cool before serving.

CHAI-SPICED SNOWDROP COOKIES

PREP TIME: 40 minutes | **COOK TIME:** 20 minutes | **TOTAL TIME:** 1 hour | **YIELD:** 50-plus cookies

I have never known a cookie to have more names than the snowdrop (aka snowball, Mexican wedding cookie, Russian tea cookie). I'm sure there are a few variations I've missed. Whatever you call them, I call them one of my favorite cookies. I didn't try snowdrops for the first time until my late twenties when my future mother-in-law brought them to a Christmas Eve gathering. I was immediately smitten with the unique texture and powdered sugar coating. Each year I make variations of this recipe, experimenting with the spice blend. But this chai version has always been one of my favorites.

FOR THE COOKIES:

8½ ounces (1½ cups) all-purpose flour

½ teaspoon kosher salt

8 ounces (16 tablespoons) unsalted butter, room temperature

2½ ounces (½ cup) confectioners' sugar

1 teaspoon pure vanilla extract

4¼ ounces (1¼ cups) almond flour

FOR THE TOPPING:

5 ounces (1 cup) confectioners' sugar

1½ teaspoons ground cinnamon

½ teaspoon ground ginger

1 teaspoon ground cardamom

1 teaspoon ground allspice

1. Preheat the oven to 325°F. Line a baking sheet with parchment paper.

2. In a small bowl, whisk the flour and salt.

3. In a stand mixer fitted with the paddle attachment, cream the butter, the ½ cup confectioners' sugar, and vanilla on high speed until light and fluffy, approximately 5 minutes.

4. Turn the mixer speed down to low and slowly add the almond flour followed by the all-purpose flour. Scrape down the sides once or twice to make sure the dough is evenly combined.

5. Use a 1 tablespoon-sized scoop to measure out the cookies. Use your hands to roll each cookie into a ball, and place on the baking sheet.

6. Chill the cookies for 20 minutes before baking for 15 to 20 minutes. While the cookies are baking, whisk the sugar topping ingredients in a bowl.

7. Remove the cookies from the oven. While they're still warm, carefully coat each cookie in the topping mixture and set aside to cool. Once the cookies have cooled, 15 to 20 minutes, toss them again in the sugar mixture.

BLOOD ORANGE CURD LINZER COOKIES

PREP TIME: 2 hours | COOK TIME: 15 minutes | TOTAL TIME: 2 hours 15 minutes
YIELD: 25 to 30 sandwich cookies

I enjoy working with shortbread for a variety of reasons, one of which being that it's completely safe to eat the egg-free cookie dough. Just being honest! But more important (maybe), shortbread dough is very forgiving when it comes to rolling out and shaping. The key is to keep it chilled but pliable. If the butter becomes too warm and soft, the dough might become difficult to roll and shape. All you have to do when this happens is place the dough in the refrigerator for fifteen minutes, or until the butter firms up again. Unlike pie and tart doughs, you can roll and reroll shortbread dough without having to worry about shrinking and elasticity. So take your time with these cookies! They are beautiful. Fruit jam or store-bought curd can be substituted to save time.

6 ounces (12 tablespoons) unsalted butter, cubed and at room temperature

2 ounces (scant ½ cup) confectioners' sugar, plus more for dusting

½ teaspoon kosher salt

1 teaspoon pure vanilla extract

10¼ ounces (1¾ cups) all-purpose flour

1 cup Blood Orange Curd (page 221)

Confectioners' sugar for dusting

1. In a stand mixer fitted with the paddle attachment, cream the butter, sugar, and salt on medium-high speed until light and fluffy, approximately 5 minutes. Add the vanilla and turn the speed to low. Slowly add the flour until the dough is evenly combined.

2. Roll the dough tightly in plastic wrap and flatten into a disc. Chill in the refrigerator for at least an hour, or until the butter firms up.

3. Place approximately one-third of the dough between two sheets of parchment paper (keep the remaining dough chilled). Roll the dough very thin, approximately ⅛ to ¼ inch thick (the thinner the better).

4. Cut into rounds with a 1½-inch cookie cutter, and place on a sheet tray covered with parchment paper. Roll the excess scraps into a ball and repeat the process until all the dough is used, including the remaining chilled dough. Use a small heart-shaped cutter to remove the center from half the rounds. Chill the dough for at least 30 minutes.

5. Preheat the oven to 350°F. Bake for 10 to 15 minutes or until lightly golden on top (bake in batches, if necessary). Allow to cool to room temperature.

6. Spread the blood orange curd onto the flat side of each uncut cookie. Top with the cut-out cookie.

7. Dust with confectioners' sugar.

PEANUT BUTTER AND JELLY
SHORTBREAD BARS

PREP TIME: 1 hour | COOK TIME: 35 minutes | TOTAL TIME: 1 hour 35 minutes | YIELD: 16 bars

These bars taste like my childhood. I've transformed the classic Concord grape jelly and peanut butter sandwich into a treat that combines two of my favorite dessert components: shortbread and homemade curd. These bars take some time and effort, but the results are so evocative, decadent, and beautiful.

5 ounces (10 tablespoons) unsalted butter, cubed and at room temperature

2½ ounces (½ cup) confectioners' sugar, plus more for dusting

½ teaspoon kosher salt

3 tablespoons creamy peanut butter

8¾ ounces (1¾ cups) all-purpose flour

1½ cups Concord Grape Curd (page 222)

1. In a stand mixer fitted with the paddle attachment, cream the butter, sugar, and salt on medium-high, until light and fluffy, approximately 5 minutes. Turn the speed to low and add the peanut butter, followed by the flour.

2. Grease a 9 x 9-inch pan with baking spray or butter and line it with parchment paper, letting the parchment paper hang over two sides of the pan. Press the dough evenly into the pan, using plastic wrap to help flatten the top. Chill the dough for at least 30 minutes.

3. Preheat the oven to 350°F. Bake for 20 minutes or until lightly golden on top. Allow to cool to room temperature.

4. Spread the Concord Grape Curd evenly on top of the shortbread. Bake at 350°F for 15 minutes. Allow to cool for 10 to 15 minutes, and then refrigerate for 20 to 30 minutes. Slice into 16 bars. Dust with confectioners' sugar before serving.

MILK CHOCOLATE DIGESTIVE BISCUITS

PREP TIME: 30 minutes | **COOK TIME:** 15 minutes | **TOTAL TIME:** 45 minutes | **YIELD:** 18 to 22 cookies

Years ago, my friend Emma introduced me to the joys of dipping McVitie's Digestive Biscuits in hot black tea. It's like the British version of dipping Oreos in milk (but I think they actually did it first). Soon I wanted to try making them from scratch, because that's what I do. They were a bit out of my element, so I found a similar recipe in Nigella Lawson's *How to Eat*, which I modified by swapping in some more easily accessible ingredients and adding the milk chocolate topping I think is essential for good dipping. One word of advice: don't omit the shortening in favor of all butter; it will change the texture of the cookies and you definitely don't want to do that. These are exactly how digestive biscuits should be—flaky, slightly dry, a bit sweet, and perfect for soaking up tea or eating on their own.

½ cup old-fashioned rolled oats

7¼ ounces (1½ cups) spelt flour

½ teaspoon kosher salt

1 teaspoon baking powder

2 tablespoons light brown sugar

¼ cup vegetable shortening, cold and cut into small pieces

2 tablespoons unsalted butter, cold and cut into small pieces

⅓ cup heavy cream

All-purpose flour for rolling out the dough

1 cup milk chocolate chips

1. Preheat the oven to 400°F. Line a baking sheet with parchment paper.

2. Add the oats, spelt flour, salt, baking powder, and sugar to a food processor and pulse several times until the oats are chopped into smaller pieces. Leave a little bit of texture to add flakiness to the cookies.

3. Move the oat mixture to a large bowl and add the shortening. Using clean hands, rub the shortening into the oat mixture until it's crumbly. When the shortening is almost completely incorporated, add the butter and do the same thing until everything is combined (as with regular biscuits, it's fine if there are some small bits of butter scattered through the dough).

4. Add the cream slowly, stirring the mixture with a spatula, until the biscuit dough comes together. Knead it in the bowl a few times.

5. Lightly flour a clean surface and roll the dough to approximately ¼-inch thickness. Using a small cookie cutter (approximately 2½ inches), cut out the biscuits and place them on the baking sheet. Reroll and cut the dough until all the dough is used.

recipe continued on page 264

6. Bake for 10 to 15 minutes, until lightly golden and just browning at the edges. Allow to cool completely.

7. When the cookies are cool, place the chocolate chips in a microwave-safe bowl. Microwave the chocolate in 15- to 30-second intervals, stirring well each time, until the chocolate is shiny and melted (this can also be done over a double boiler).

8. Use a pastry brush to generously brush the melted chocolate onto the cookies. Place the cookies in the refrigerator for approximately 10 minutes to set the chocolate.

9. Serve the biscuits with black tea for dipping.

PISTACHIO CARDAMOM BAKLAVA

PREP TIME: 4 hours 30 minutes (mostly inactive) | **COOK TIME:** 1 hour
TOTAL TIME: 5 hours 30 minutes (mostly inactive) | **YIELD:** 30 to 40 pieces

Years ago when I was working a desk job, I had an "aha" moment about food. It had been so long since I had seriously cooked or baked for pleasure and I think I had forgotten how amazing homemade desserts could be. Someone brought a large plate of freshly prepared baklava to the office and it seemed like one of the best things I had ever tasted. I wanted to know how to bake from scratch like that. Phyllo dough can dry out quickly. To prevent this, place a clean, slightly dampened dish towel over the unused sheets while preparing the dessert.

1 cup honey, preferably orange blossom

1½ cups water

1¾ cups plus 3 tablespoons granulated sugar

2 tablespoons fresh-squeezed lemon juice (approximately 1 lemon)

Lemon zest (approximately 1 inch peel)

4 cardamom pods, smashed

1¼ teaspoon ground cardamom

2 cups shelled, unsalted pistachios, toasted and finely chopped

1 teaspoon ground cinnamon

¼ teaspoon kosher salt

8 ounces (16 tablespoons) unsalted butter, melted

1 pound frozen phyllo dough

1. In a large saucepan, combine the honey, water, 1¾ cups sugar, lemon juice, zest, cardamom pods, and ¼ teaspoon of the ground cardamom. Bring to a simmer over medium heat, and then reduce the heat to medium-low. Simmer for 6 to 8 minutes, stirring periodically. Remove from the heat and cool for 15 minutes. Strain, cover, and chill in the refrigerator.

2. In a food processor, combine the remaining 1 teaspoon ground cardamom, pistachios, 3 tablespoons sugar, cinnamon, and salt. Pulse several times until the nuts are coarsely chopped and the ingredients are evenly combined.

3. Preheat the oven to 350°F. Brush a 9 x 13-inch baking dish with some of the butter.

4. Layer 8 pieces of phyllo in the dish, brushing with melted butter between each layer. Sprinkle one-third of the nut mixture evenly over the phyllo. Layer 5 additional pieces of phyllo into the dish, again brushing each layer with butter. Top evenly with one-third of the nut mixture. Repeat this process with 5 more sheets of phyllo and the remaining one-third of the nut mixture. Finish by layering 8 pieces of phyllo into the dish, brushing with melted butter between each layer.

recipe continued on page 267

5. Cut into the baklava lengthwise to make strips, approximately 1½ inches wide. Next, make diagonal slices, approximately 1½ inches apart, to create a diamond pattern.

6. Bake for 45 to 55 minutes, until the phyllo is golden brown on top. Remove from the oven and slowly pour the chilled syrup over the hot baklava. Allow to soak for at least 4 hours, or overnight before serving.

PIES, TARTS, AND FRUIT DESSERTS

BLACKBERRY HAND PIES

PREP TIME: 2 hours (mostly inactive) | **COOK TIME:** 30 minutes
TOTAL TIME: 2 hours 30 minutes (mostly inactive) | **YIELD:** 8 pies

There's something very satisfying about a freshly baked hand pie straight out of the oven. While there is beauty in the perfection of a woven lattice pie crust, there is something equally gorgeous about crisp, golden, individually portioned pies with juices oozing out the sides. It's the imperfections that make each little pie so lovely and appetizing. These pies taste like summer to me. Fresh blackberries are one of my favorite seasonal fruits for baking pies, but you could substitute blueberries, raspberries, or strawberries (any berry, really).

FOR THE DOUGH:
12 ounces (2½ cups) all-purpose flour

¼ cup granulated sugar

½ teaspoon kosher salt

8 ounces (16 tablespoons) unsalted butter, cold and cut into small pieces

⅓ cup cold water

FOR THE FILLING:
2 cups (10 ounces) fresh blackberries

1½ teaspoons cornstarch

2 teaspoons granulated sugar, or more to taste

1 teaspoon fresh-squeezed lemon juice

¼ teaspoon pure vanilla extract

Pinch of kosher salt

FOR THE TOPPING:
1 large egg

1 tablespoon water

2 to 3 teaspoons turbinado sugar

TO PREPARE THE DOUGH:

1. Place the flour, granulated sugar, and salt in a food processor. Pulse several times to combine the ingredients. Add the butter and pulse until the mixture looks like coarse cornmeal (a few larger pieces of butter are fine). With the machine running, add the water and mix until the dough just begins to come together. Do not overmix.

recipe continued on page 270

2. Wrap the dough in plastic wrap, flatten into a disk, and place in the refrigerator for a minimum of 1 hour (see note).

TO PREPARE THE FILLING:

1. Place the blackberries, cornstarch, granulated sugar, lemon juice, vanilla, and salt in a medium bowl. Cover and place in the refrigerator for 25 minutes, stirring periodically to release the juices. Use a potato masher to gently mash the berries, leaving some larger pieces intact.

TO ASSEMBLE THE PIES:

1. Preheat the oven to 400°F. Line a baking sheet with parchment paper.

2. On a lightly floured surface, roll the dough to approximately ¼-inch thickness. Use a 4-inch round cookie cutter to cut 16 rounds. Before rerolling any scraps (if necessary), allow the dough to chill in the refrigerator for at least 15 minutes.

3. To prepare the egg wash, in a small bowl, briefly whisk the egg with 1 tablespoon water and a pinch of salt.

4. Brush the outer rim of one of the dough rounds with a light coating of egg wash. Place approximately 1 tablespoon of pie filling in the center of the dough and immediately cover with a second round. Use a fork to press the edges of the dough together all the way around. Brush egg wash liberally on top and sprinkle with turbinado sugar. Use a knife to vent 3 small holes on top. Repeat with the remaining ingredients.

5. Bake for 27 to 30 minutes, until the pies are golden brown on top. Allow to cool briefly before serving.

Note: The dough can be prepared up to 48 hours in advance.

GRAPEFRUIT PIE

PREP TIME: 2 hours 5 minutes (mostly inactive) | **COOK TIME:** 20 minutes
TOTAL TIME: 2 hours 25 minutes (mostly inactive) | **YIELD:** 10 to 12 servings

Key lime pie is one of my favorite summer desserts. It's tart, it's custard, and it's reminiscent of curd. It is the inspiration for this grapefruit pie, because I think we need more custard-based pies in the world. I find grapefruits to be shamefully underused in desserts. They have a level of bitterness that adds balance to desserts in the same way that caramel does. A few notes about the recipe: I've used a pâte brisée tart dough as the base, which is delicate and flaky. If you want to save time and simplify the recipe to just five ingredients, store-bought pie dough will work well here. Also, please note that this is not a deep-dish pie recipe. Use a shallow 9 x 1-inch or 9 x 2-inch pie or tart pan.

5 ounces (1 cup) all-purpose flour, plus more for dusting

3 ounces (6 tablespoons) unsalted butter, cubed and cold

½ teaspoon kosher salt

3 tablespoons cold water

1 (14-ounce) can sweetened condensed milk

1¼ cup fresh-squeezed grapefruit juice

2 large eggs

1 large egg yolk

1. Place the flour, butter, and salt in a food processor. Pulse the machine on and off until the mixture is crumbly. While the machine is running, slowly add the water until just combined (do not overmix). Wrap the dough in plastic wrap and flatten into a disk. Chill for at least 2 hours, or overnight (see note).

2. Allow the dough to rest at room temperature for 5 minutes. On a lightly floured surface, roll the dough to approximately ¼ inch. Carefully place the dough into a shallow pie pan. Place the pan back in the refrigerator and chill for 30 minutes.

3. Preheat the oven to 400°F. Place the pie pan on a baking sheet. Use a fork to poke holes throughout the bottom of the dough to prevent air bubbles from forming. Line the pie pan with foil and cover with uncooked beans. Bake for 20 minutes, removing the beans and foil for the last 5 minutes. Allow to cool while preparing the other ingredients.

4. Preheat the oven to 325°F. Place the prepared pie crust on a baking sheet.

recipe continued on page 273

5. In a large bowl, whisk the condensed milk, grapefruit juice, eggs, and egg yolk.

6. Pour the custard into the pie shell, leaving at least ¼ inch around the top.

7. Carefully place the baking sheet with the pie into the oven and bake for 25 to 30 minutes. It will still be wobbly, but should be slightly firmer to the touch.

8. Chill in the refrigerator for at least 2 hours, or overnight to set the custard. Serve chilled or slightly above room temperature.

Note: Dough can be made up to 72 hours in advance.

NECTARINE PIE

PREP TIME: 1 hour 30 minutes (mostly inactive) | **COOK TIME:** 1 hour
TOTAL TIME: 2 hours 30 minutes (mostly inactive) | **YIELD:** 10 to 12 servings

For some reason nectarines seem to take a backseat to peaches in the culinary world, but I can't figure out why. Nectarines are fantastic and they make a killer pie. As with peaches, it's worth it to try and get your hands on local fruit while it's in season. The flavor is above and beyond anything you'll find at the grocery store. And if you're going to take the time to make a pie from scratch, you definitely want to maximize the results! Note that granulated sugar may be substituted for the turbinado sugar.

FOR THE DOUGH:

12 ounces (2½ cups) all-purpose flour

¼ cup granulated sugar

½ teaspoon kosher salt

8 ounces (16 tablespoons) unsalted butter, cold and cut into small pieces

⅓ cup cold water

FOR THE FILLING:

3½ pounds ripe nectarines (6 to 7 medium)

1½ tablespoons fresh-squeezed lemon juice (approximately ½ lemon)

¼ cup granulated sugar

¼ cup light brown sugar

¼ teaspoon ground cinnamon

⅛ teaspoon fresh nutmeg

⅛ teaspoon kosher salt

3 tablespoons cornstarch

ADDITIONAL:

1 tablespoon milk or heavy cream

1 tablespoon raw turbinado sugar

PREPARE THE DOUGH:

1. Place the flour, granulated sugar, and salt in a food processor. Pulse the dry ingredients several times to mix. Add the butter and pulse the machine until the mixture looks like coarse cornmeal (a few larger pieces of butter are fine). With the machine running, add the water and mix until the dough just begins to come together.

2. Divide the dough into ⅓ and ⅔ portions, wrap in plastic wrap, and flatten into disks. Place in the refrigerator for a minimum of 1 hour (see note).

PREPARE THE FILLING:

1. Bring a large pot of water to a boil. Fill a large bowl with ice water. On the bottom of each nectarine, slice a 1-inch X shape (cut only the skin, not the fruit). Using a slotted spoon, carefully add a few of the nectarines to the boiling water. After 30 to 60 seconds, you should see the skin separating slightly from the fruit. Use the slotted spoon to remove the nectarines and dunk into the ice water bath. Repeat with the remaining nectarines.

2. Peel the skin from the nectarines and discard. If any of the skins are stubborn, use a small paring knife to assist

recipe continued on page 276

in the peeling. Slice the fruit in half and remove the pits. Place the nectarines flat side down and cut into thin slices. Transfer the sliced nectarines into a large bowl and toss with the lemon juice.

3. In a small bowl, stir the granulated and brown sugars, cinnamon, nutmeg, salt, and cornstarch. Add to the nectarines, stirring to combine. Set aside.

ASSEMBLE THE PIE:

1. Preheat the oven to 425°F.

2. On a generously floured surface, roll out the larger portion of dough to 12 to 13 inches in diameter (flour the top of the dough as well). Carefully place in a 9-inch pie pan. There should be a slight overhang. Top with the nectarine filling.

3. Re-flour the surface and roll out the smaller portion of dough to approximately 10 inches in diameter. Use a pizza slicer to cut 8 even strips. Layer the strips in a decorative lattice pattern. Cut off any excess overhang from the strips and then fold the bottom overhang over the strips. Use a fork to gently crimp the edge of the crust all around.

4. Brush the milk evenly over the dough and sprinkle with the turbinado sugar.

5. Place the pie pan on a baking sheet and place in the oven. Cook for 20 minutes and then lower the oven temperature to 375°F. Bake for an additional 35 to 40 minutes, or until the crust is brown and the filling is bubbly.

6. Allow to cool completely to room temperature before slicing (the filling will thicken as it cools).

Note: Dough can be made up to 48 hours in advance.

PLUM GALETTE WITH MASCARPONE AND ROSEMARY

PREP TIME: 2 hours | **COOK TIME:** 25 minutes | **TOTAL TIME:** 2 hours 25 minutes
YIELD: 8 to 10 servings

When I was in culinary school, one of the pastry chefs described a galette as a "rustic tart" and then added, "I love the word 'rustic.' It means it doesn't have to be pretty." She had a point, in the sense that when using tart molds, I often spend quite a bit of time making sure the dough is perfectly formed. Galettes are much easier, but their imperfections are what make them beautiful. They're great for beginners and experts alike. When selecting plums for this recipe, avoid overly ripened plums. They will be too watery and will not hold their shape as well when sliced. Look for firm plums that give just slightly when pressed.

5 ounces (1 cup) all-purpose flour, plus more for dusting

½ teaspoon kosher salt

1 teaspoon fresh rosemary

3 ounces (6 tablespoons) unsalted butter, cold and cut into small pieces

2 to 3 tablespoons cold water

3 to 4 firm, ripe red plums

½ cup mascarpone cheese

2 tablespoons apricot jam

Ground black pepper (optional)

1. Add the flour, salt, and rosemary to a food processor. Pulse several times to chop the rosemary and combine the ingredients. Add the butter and continue pulsing until the mixture is crumbly. Slowly add the water with the machine running until the dough forms a ball. Wrap the dough in plastic wrap and flatten into a disk. Chill for at least 2 hours, or overnight (see note).

2. Preheat the oven to 375°F and line a baking sheet with parchment paper. On a lightly floured surface, roll the dough into a circle approximately 9 inches in diameter. Use a knife or pizza cutter to clean up the edges and move the dough to the baking sheet. Place in the refrigerator.

3. Line a plate with paper towels. Slice the plums in half and carefully remove the pits. Place each half face down on a cutting board and slice thinly. Place the slices on the paper towels to drain any excess liquid, and repeat with the remaining plums.

4. Remove the baking sheet from the refrigerator and spread the mascarpone evenly onto the dough, leaving an inch of untouched border all the way around. Layer the plum slices

recipe continued on page 279

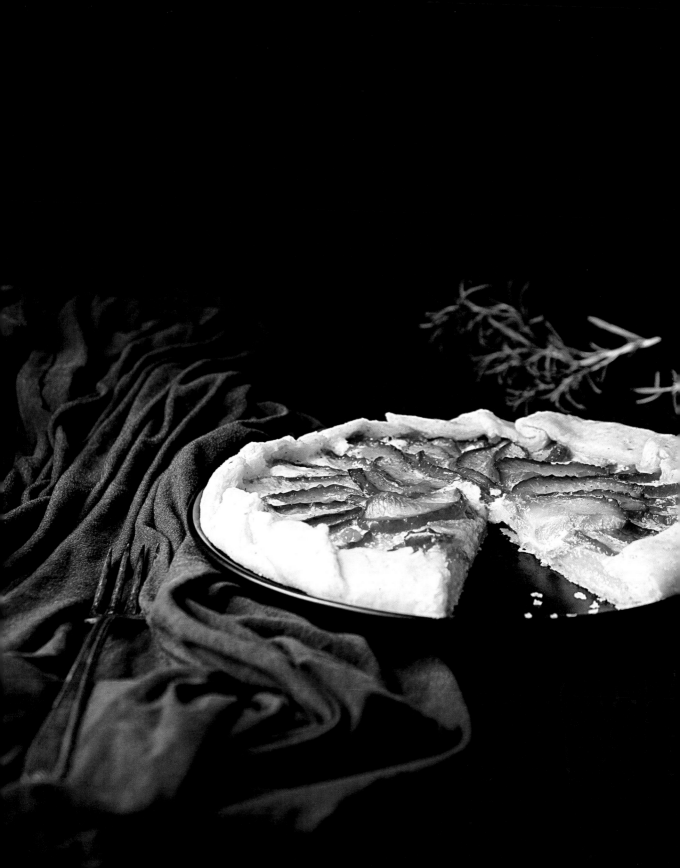

in a decorative circular pattern, starting with the outer layer and finishing with an inner layer. Fold the excess dough over the plum slices to create a tightly formed tart.

5. Bake for 22 to 25 minutes, or until the dough is cooked and the center is bubbly. When the galette has almost finished baking, place the apricot jam in a small ramekin and microwave for 20 to 30 seconds to thin.

6. Remove the galette from the oven. Use a pastry brush to dab the apricot jam evenly over the top of the fruit, taking care not to disturb the shape of the plums.

7. Add a light sprinkling of pepper to the top, if using.

8. Allow the tart to cool until it's lukewarm, or at room temperature before serving.

Note: Dough can be made up to 72 hours in advance.

GOAT CHEESE MOUSSE
WITH ROASTED BLUEBERRIES

PREP TIME: 15 minutes | **COOK TIME:** 12 minutes | **TOTAL TIME:** 27 minutes | **YIELD:** 6 to 8 servings

With only four ingredients, this is a quick and light dessert. Goat cheese adds an unexpected tartness to the mousse, and the roasted berries provide a sweet, colorful contrast. It looks beautiful when presented in little decorative jars, but can be served in cups, wineglasses, or bowls. For best results, serve the mousse within two to three hours.

5 ounces soft goat cheese, room temperature

1½ cups heavy cream, cold

¼ cup granulated sugar

18 ounces blueberries (approximately 3 cups)

1. Preheat the oven to 400°F and line a baking sheet with aluminum foil. Place the goat cheese in a large bowl and set aside.

2. In a stand mixer with the whisk attachment (or with a large metal bowl and a handheld whisk), whip the heavy cream and sugar to a stiff peak.

3. Spoon half of the whipped cream into the bowl with the goat cheese and vigorously whisk until smooth. Add the remaining whipped cream and gently fold to combine. Cover and chill in the refrigerator.

4. Place the blueberries on the baking sheet and place in the oven. Roast in 4-minute intervals, gently shaking the pan each time, for 12 to 16 minutes. Allow to cool for 5 to 10 minutes.

5. Spoon the mousse into small bowls and top with the roasted blueberries.

GRILLED PEARS WITH HONEY ROQUEFORT WHIPPED CREAM

PREP TIME: 2 hours 10 minutes (mostly inactive) | **COOK TIME:** 5 minutes
TOTAL TIME: 2 hours 15 minutes (mostly inactive) | **YIELD:** 4 to 8 servings

This is a wonderful summer dessert. No oven is required, it's not heavy or overly filling, and the sweetness level is just right. The trick to grilling pears (or any fruit) is to not touch them after placing them on the grill. Give them a chance to develop grill marks and absorb the smokiness. Salty Roquefort cheese adds a fun savory element.

1 cup heavy whipping cream

¼ cup Roquefort cheese

2 tablespoons honey

4 firm, ripe Bartlett pears

¼ cup vegetable oil

½ cup toasted pecans, chopped

1. In a small saucepan, heat ½ cup of the cream with the Roquefort and honey over medium heat. Stir until the mixture begins to simmer and the cheese is completely incorporated without any lumps. Add the remaining ½ cup cream, cover, and refrigerate until cold (see note). Once cold, whip the cream by hand or in a stand mixer fitted with the whisk attachment. The cream should form a stiff peak.

2. Preheat a grill on medium-high heat for several minutes, until very hot. Slice the pears in half from stem to root and use a melon baller or small spoon to scoop out the seeds. Brush oil liberally onto the cut side of the pears.

3. Carefully place each pear on the grill, cut side down. Close the lid and grill for 4 minutes. Use tongs to remove and let cool until the pears are warm or room temperature.

4. Scoop a dollop of Roquefort whipped cream onto each pear half and top with a sprinkle of pecans. Serve immediately.

Note: Roquefort whipped cream can be made up to 24 hours in advance.

CANDY AND DRINKS

CHOCOLATE MALT TRUFFLES

PREP TIME: 3 hours 15 minutes (mostly inactive) | **COOK TIME:** 5 minutes
TOTAL TIME: 3 hours 20 minutes (mostly inactive) | **YIELD:** 15 to 30 truffles, depending on size

Homemade truffles are a simple dessert with just a few ingredients. They're a wonderful gift for chocolate lovers! One of the common issues people run into while making these is that they can be slightly difficult to roll, even if the ganache is thoroughly chilled in advance. While it's not essential, I recommend using kitchen-safe gloves to roll the truffles. Not only will it keep your hands clean, it will create a small barrier between the chocolate and your body's natural heat.

FOR THE TRUFFLES:

8 ounces bittersweet chocolate, chopped

½ cup heavy cream

¼ cup plus 1 tablespoon malted milk powder

FOR THE COATING:

1 tablespoon plus 1 teaspoon unsweetened cocoa powder

¼ cup malted milk powder

1. Place the chocolate in a medium bowl and set aside.

2. To form the ganache, heat the cream in a small saucepan over medium-high heat. As it begins to simmer, whisk in the malt powder, stirring until evenly combined. Once the cream has come to a boil, remove from heat and pour over the chocolate. Allow the mixture to sit for 2 to 3 minutes. With a heatproof spatula, stir until the chocolate has melted completely and the mixture is combined.

3. Allow the ganache to cool slightly, then cover the bowl with a towel and chill in the refrigerator for 3 hours or overnight.

4. In a small bowl, whisk the cocoa powder and malt powder for the topping.

5. Use a tablespoon to scoop out some ganache and quickly roll into a ball. Body heat will cause the ganache to start melting quickly; kitchen gloves will provide a barrier and make the rolling process easier. Toss in the topping and set aside. Repeat until all of the chocolate has been used.

6. The truffles will soften as they warm, so keep them refrigerated before serving.

SPICED CANDIED ORANGE PEEL

PREP TIME: 5 minutes | COOK TIME: 2 hours 15 minutes | TOTAL TIME: 2 hours 20 minutes | YIELD: 4 cups

Candied orange peel is one of my favorite homemade gifts to give during the holiday season. I usually have to double up on the batch so I have enough for myself as well as others. There are many recipes that suggest dipping candied orange peel in melted chocolate, but I've always preferred them plain, especially this spiced version. Your kitchen will smell wonderful while the zest is simmering with the spices. Because the peels take a while to candy and need to be monitored regularly, I typically prepare this recipe while watching a favorite holiday movie. I set a kitchen timer so I remember to stir the peels periodically. The recipe involves a bit of effort, but the results are truly worth it. Save the leftover spiced syrup to add to drinks.

4 medium oranges

3½ cups granulated sugar

2 cups water

1 vanilla bean, split down the middle

10 whole black peppercorns

6 cardamom pods, smashed

4 cinnamon sticks

3 whole cloves

1. Cut the oranges into quarters. Use a spoon to scoop out the fruit and set aside, taking care to leave as much of the white pith attached to the peel as possible. Slice the peel into thin slices, about ¼ inch thick or smaller.

2. Place the orange peels in a large saucepan and cover with cold water. Bring to a boil and then simmer for 3 minutes. Drain and repeat this process two more times using fresh water each time (do not skip this step, as it removes the bitterness from the peel).

3. Clean the saucepan thoroughly to remove any residual bitterness. Add the water, 2½ cups of the sugar, the vanilla bean, peppercorns, cardamom pods, cinnamon sticks, and cloves. Bring to a boil, stirring occasionally to dissolve the sugar. Reduce to a simmer and add the orange peels. Simmer on low heat, stirring every 10 to 15 minutes, until the fruit becomes slightly translucent, 1½ to 2 hours.

4. Line a baking sheet with parchment paper or aluminum foil and top with a cooling rack. Using tongs, remove the orange peels from the syrup, shake off any excess liquid, and transfer to the rack to finish draining. Let the candied orange peels dry overnight.

5. Toss with the remaining 1 cup sugar before serving.

BLOOD ORANGE GIN AND TONIC

PREP TIME: 5 minutes | TOTAL TIME: 5 minutes | YIELD: 2 servings

I'm not a big drinker; I mainly use alcohol in recipes. When I do drink, I tend to stick with white wine or a few specialty cocktails. Gin and tonics are always in my rotation. They're refreshing, citrusy, and just slightly sweet from the tonic. The key to a good G and T, as with many cocktails, is to use quality ingredients. Cheap gin tastes like rubbing alcohol; Bombay Sapphire is a good-quality gin. The standard tonic brands are nothing special. If you're willing to spend just a little bit more, it will make a huge difference! If you live near a Whole Foods, its 365 brand is very reasonably priced. Fever Tree is another great option that can be found at many liquor and grocery stores. I tend to go heavy on the lime juice, which is why I recommend adding it to taste. While fresh-squeezed blood orange juice will taste best in this drink, you can use bottled varieties if scaling up the recipe. Just try to find juices with no added ingredients. In a pinch, regular fresh-squeezed or bottled orange juice will also get the job done.

1 cup fresh-squeezed blood orange juice (2 to 4 blood oranges)

1 cup good-quality tonic water

2 shots good-quality gin

½ to 1 lime, juiced

Lime wedges, for garnish

1. Combine the blood orange juice, tonic water, and gin.

2. Add the lime juice to taste.

3. Serve over ice. Garnish with lime wedges.

SPIKED HOT CHOCOLATE WITH SALTED CARAMEL WHIPPED CREAM

PREP TIME: 3 hours 10 minutes (mostly inactive) | **COOK TIME:** 10 minutes
TOTAL TIME: 3 hours 20 minutes (mostly inactive) | **YIELD:** 3 to 4 servings

This is a seriously decadent drink, one that's perfect for cold-weather months. Sure, the alcohol can be omitted. But bittersweet chocolate, bourbon, and salted caramel are a winning trio. You can speed up the time required for chilling the salted caramel cream by using an ice bath. Before cooking the caramel, fill a large bowl with ice and some water. After the caramel and cream have been combined and removed from the heat, place the saucepan directly over the ice bath and stir periodically while allowing the cream to cool. This will cut down the time required to finish chilling in the refrigerator by half or more.

¼ cup granulated sugar

1 tablespoon water

½ teaspoon kosher salt

1 cup heavy whipping cream

3 cups whole milk

6 ounces bittersweet chocolate, chopped

½ teaspoon pure vanilla extract

¼ cup bourbon

1. In a medium saucepan, heat the sugar, water, and salt over medium heat until the sugar is dissolved. Allow the sugar to continue cooking, keeping a close eye on it, until it starts to turn golden brown. Once it begins to caramelize, it will continue to darken quickly. Let the sugar get as dark as possible without burning for best results. Once the caramel is a dark amber color, remove the pan from the heat and pour the heavy cream down the side of the saucepan. The caramel will splatter before temporarily seizing up, so be very careful to avoid burns. Move the pan back onto the burner and use a heatproof spatula to stir the caramel and cream until evenly combined. Remove from the heat and allow to cool for 5 to 10 minutes, stirring periodically.

2. Pour the caramel into a clean bowl and cover with plastic wrap, pressing the film directly against the cream to prevent a skin from forming. Allow to chill until very cold, several hours or overnight.

3. In a stand mixer fitted with the whisk attachment, or using a large bowl and a whisk, whip the caramel cream until it reaches a medium peak. Set aside.

4. In a medium saucepan, heat the milk over medium heat. When the milk is steaming hot but not yet simmering, remove from the heat and add the chocolate. Allow the mixture to sit for a few minutes until the chocolate has melted. Vigorously whisk in the vanilla and bourbon, and briefly return to the heat until the desired serving temperature is reached. Pour into mugs and top each with a dollop of whipped cream.

*All you need is love. But a little
chocolate now and then doesn't hurt.*
—Charles M. Schulz

WITH GRATITUDE

Family is everything to me, and none of this would matter without them. To Jeff: I couldn't have done any of this without you. Thank you for believing in me, and for giving me the courage to step out of my comfort zone and chase my dreams. To Mom and Dad: thank you for being the most amazing parents, and for always being supportive of me no matter what. To Dave and Dee: thank you for your love and encouragement. To Rob and Alison: thanks for letting us stay at your beach house while I was finishing the book. It was more helpful than you can possibly imagine!

To Shannon Clark Early, Carrie Burrill, Joanne Ozug, Caroline Hurley, Jackie Dodd, and Carolyn Ketchum: thank you for your friendship, and for helping me stay sane during an insane year. I am incredibly lucky to know all of you. You inspire me with your kindness and creativity.

Thanks to Monica Bhide, Casey Benedict, and Robyn Webb for mentoring me over the past few years. A big thank-you to Deanie Jennings for helping me keep everything in perspective. To Samantha Hegre: thanks for helping me stay organized. And thank you to Julie Wender and Allison Rashkin for showing me that burning off the cupcake calories is *almost* as fun as eating them.

Thank you to Janis Donnaud for helping me navigate the strange and unusual world of cookbooks. Thanks to everyone at Simon and Schuster for taking a chance on me, including Jeremie Ruby-Strauss, Carolyn Reidy, Louise Burke, Jennifer Bergstrom, Nina Cordes, Jaime Putorti, Liz Psaltis, and Jean Anne Rose.

Thanks to all of the companies who have helped me along the way, including California Strawberries, Bob's Red Mill, Stemilt Growers, Wisconsin Cheese Company, Vermont Creamery, First We Eat, Zoku, eHow, Zengo Cycle, and From The Farmer.

Lots of love to everyone who reads *Savory Simple*. Your kind words are motivating in so many ways. This book would not exist without you.

Many people were willing to test my recipes in advance of the book publication. Their honest feedback was so helpful and truly made this a better cookbook. They caught omissions and typos, and you will now know to remove the frittata from the oven when the eggs are no longer jiggling as opposed to giggling. A heartfelt thank-you to Amy Flannigan, Andrea Paun, Brian and Jess Minkove, Cayley Rice, Deseree Kazda, Erin Burkert, Gerry Spears, Jen Schall, Jenni Field, Jennifer Bennett, Laura Kumin, Lauree Ostrofsky, Lauren Keating, Shannon Hoffman, Sherron Watson, Susan Williams, Valerie Catrice, Xani Poldony, Alison Arsenault, Barbara Maekawa, Betsy Payne Watson, Carol Cooke, Carol Rusby, Chaya Rivky Adler, Cheri K. Huff, Cynthia Shepard, Dana L. Pulver, Erin Knack, Jennifer Johnson, Jenny Bullistron, Julie Coleman, Karen A. Fessler, Karen Abela, Kim Jidas, Kimberly Catapano, Kimberly Porter, Kristi Akers, Linda Reed, Maria Fusco, Martha Gallant, Michelle Martinez, Monica Pomeroy, Nicole Bosley, Norma Dimsey, Paula Bernardi, Rachel Gue Roe, Roopali Bhargava, Sandra deMiranda, and Tawny Godin.

Finally, thanks to Xanax and Ben & Jerry's Chubby Hubby for helping me get through the really stressful weeks. Is that TMI?

INDEX

Note: Page numbers in *italics* refer to illustrations.

ABOUT THE AUTHOR

Jennifer Farley is the writer, food photographer, and stylist behind *Savory Simple*, a blog dedicated to everyday gourmet recipes for the home cook. She believes that with an understanding of basic techniques and a willingness to experiment, anyone can be an amazing cook. Jennifer graduated from the Culinary Arts program at L'Academie de Cuisine in Gaithersburg, Maryland, and has worked professionally as a line cook, pastry chef, and cooking instructor. Her work has been featured by Williams-Sonoma, *Better Homes and Gardens*, *Parade*, Food52, *The Kitchn*, and *Food & Wine*. Jennifer lives in Washington, DC, with her husband, Jeff, and her cat, Sofi.

www.SavorySimple.net

www.JenniferFarleyPhotography.com